All the
Saints Agree

By

Dr. Lydia A. Woods

CWP

Channing & Watt Publishers
Peoria, AZ

Channing & Watt Publishers
Peoria, Arizona
www.channingandwatt.com

For information contact:
info@channingandwatt.com

Front Cover Photo/Book Design by
JD Woods Consulting

Back Cover Photo by
William C. Terry

Printed in the United States of America

ISBN-13: 978-1-941200-18-6
LCCN: 2001088530

Other Publications
by Dr. Lydia A. Woods

Poems by Revelation
For the Edification of the Saints
Food for Saints
Let Those With Ears…
Conversations with the Saints
All the Saints Agree
Acceptance with Joy
Those Bible Women
Those Bible Characters
The Joy of the Lord
Made in the Fire
Under the Rainbow

Dedicated with Love to

William C. Terry

Acknowledgements

I want to give special thanks to my sister for her cover design and many hours of formatting for publication. Her unique skills and talents are invaluable to me!

Thank you, Holy Spirit, for using my humble vessel
and letting me put my name on these words.

Table of Contents

Poems

Scriptural References

Introduction

Under the inspiration of the Holy Spirit, I began writing Christian Poetry. The Spirit would "overshadow" me as the old folk used to say and I would copy down what was given. The Spirit would leave and return again several months later. This continued for about five years until there was enough poetry for me to begin questioning the Lord as to the purpose of this gift. He instructed me to begin to put the poems all in one place in an orderly format. The first book, entitled "Poems by Revelation," was the result. While putting the book in publishable form the Spirit became extremely active which led to a second collection of poems and thus, I began on the unlikely path of author/publisher.

These collections of poems are inspired by the lessons which the Lord has been teaching me over years of walking with Him. Many poems are inspired by uplifting and stimulating conversations with God's precious saints and others are born out of frustration from ungodliness and ignorance of God's Word which exist around me.

In reading, I hope you will find poems which speak to your heart and express what you have experienced on your walk with the Father. The writing of these poems allows me an outlet of expression as the Lord tempers and prepares me for my calling.

Poems

Above All

John 14:13; 1 John 5:14; Ephesians 3:10 (KJV)
Scriptural Reference on page 90

Why is it written that He will do,
Above all that we ask Him to?

Also, above that which we can think, also,
I've often wondered about this, I want to know.

I've figured out that He's placed every desire in my heart,
That it did not originate on my small part.

The Lord placed those desires so long ago,
Before I was born in fact – didn't you know?

So, if He has placed those desires there,
He is also able to fulfill them with love and care.

But He holds a little back for Himself,
To surprise His children and bless them with His wealth.

That's the part about "Above All," that we can think or ask,
He saves the extra special part until the very last.

He has wealth, that even our minds can't comprehend,
And He likes to play the "Above Card," in the end.

He enjoys seeing our joy and delight,
It makes our testimony glorious and extraordinarily bright.

We can't wait to tell just what He has done,
We want to run and share it with everyone.

That He didn't just do, what we had asked,
But He went beyond that wee small task.

He never does things tiny or infinitely small,
But He is in the business of – Above All!

Be Still!

Psalms 46:10 (KJV)
Scriptural Reference on page 91

As a child of God, He often says to me,
Child "Be Still," just wait and see.
I hate it when He says, "Be Still,"
Cause' my flesh is jumpin' – that's against my will.

He means, "Be Still," in your flesh and mouth and mind,
Just sit yourself down on your behind.

The nature of a child is to move, move about,
Running here and there trying to figure things out.
Just what to do about this and that,
That's true about kids and that is just a fact.

So, when the Father says to "Be Still,"
He means that we are to submit our Will,
The very thing that you want to do,
Put it on the shelf, like He told you to.

He has a plan for the problem already in hand,
Before you were born, because He "Is the Man,"
In heaven and earth it's always His Will,
So will you just sit down and "Be Still!"

A Bible Character

Luke 22:47, 57, 60; 23:21-34; Mark 15:1, 10-11, 16:1; Matthew 21:24;
1 Peter 2:9 (KJV) Scriptural Reference on page 92

I've heard the Holy Book called the, "Living Word,"
It lives and breathes, and strains to be heard.
And I heard a Saint say, I'd like to be,
A Bible character for all to see.

No sooner said, than the chance came their way,
The Word leapt from the page to the everyday.
And all of a sudden that Word came alive,
The Holy Spirit had heard, and opportunity arrived.

It's an honor to be on the battlefield,
In the perilous days when warfare is real.
We'll all get our chance to stand for Christ,
And prove to everyone that we're bought with a price.

Which character will you be on that Bible stage,
If the casting is done and war is waged?
Are you Judas, who comes with kisses by night,
Or Pilate who washes the blood out of sight?

Are you in the crowd crying crucify Him,
Or Peter who denies that he is His friend?
Or the soldiers who cast lots for His garment in greed
Or the wicked leaders who arranged the deed?

Are you one of the twelve who walked with Him,
But couldn't be found when the evening grew dim?
Were you one of the women, He delivered from sin,
But remembered that He said, "He would rise again?"

Even though they were afraid, they went to the tomb,
To give honor to their Lord and His body groom.
Will you be counted with the very few,
Who waited on the Lord as their hope grew?

And believed all He'd said would come true,
That He would return for me and you
And in the meantime, while we're on earth,
Washed in His blood, a child of new birth.

Just check yourself out in every way,
And see which role you'll play today.
Could they cast you for peculiar people indeed,
The Royal Priesthood and Child of His seed?

Called by His name and set aside,
The Temple of God, let His Spirit abide.
In the beauty of Holiness tried and true,
Let His Spirit be found in me and you.

A Bible Character

A Blessing – Not a Curse!

Psalms 127:3-5 (KJV)
Scriptural Reference on page 95

It is written, children are a Blessing not a curse,
But a bunch of kids – What could be worse?

They suck your time and money, kill your dreams,
It's a long hard haul, and so it seems.

That for the present I wonder how and why,
These kids will bless me by and by.

To sacrifice your life's blood - And children just take,
At times it seems having them was a big mistake.

If you've walked that path you know what I mean,
Especially, if you have survived the teens!

Each stage brings joys, frustrations, and fears,
Will they ever mature -- These little dears?

But if you ask me if I'd do it all again,
Without a doubt I would answer, yes, my friend.

Cause when I beheld my new precious grandson,
I knew deep joy and gladness had really begun.

I never realized that the next step would be,
Generations through my seed for me to see,

A strange feeling of happiness in God's plan,
To bring generations through the seed of man,

Being a door to life, is worth all the pain,
The plan is quite amazing and simple to explain.

That a bunch of kids - What could be worse?
Children are a blessing -- Not a curse!

- Conversation with Mr. Gene Wideman

But For Your Praying Saints

Ephesians 6:18; 1 Thessalonians 5:17; James 5:16 (KJV)
Scriptural Reference on page 96

Look out Satan 'cause you've been uncovered,
The truth has been told by my spiritual brother,
Frank Peretti is the Saint that's blessed me well.
He reveals what's going on in the pit of hell.

When he reads his book, "*This Present Darkness*" on cassette,
I'm telling you Saints you will never regret.
Listening to this book will spiritually educate you,
It will give you insight on just what to do.

His book is all about Satan's demons as they plot and plan,
To destroy God's Saints and steal the souls of man.
But don't despair the Lord's warriors are in place.
He dispatches angelic forces and they're on the case.

Their weapons are mighty for strongholds come down,
And they are powered by Saints that aren't playing around.
He speaks of Saints who know just what to do,
Using the power of prayer as they were commanded to.

As those mighty prayers ascend to the throne.
They empower the angels and they make right the wrong.
They can take out Satanic demons left and right,
They make quick work of them in this spiritual fight.

My daughter and I play the tape over and over again,
We love to hear the ending, when the angels win,
And then there's our favorite line in all of the book,
As the demon breathes his last and takes one long look,

At the captain of the host his angelic enemy,
Now here's the part that thrills my daughter and me.
Before he is vanquished – he speaks deep and faint,
But for your praying saints.

Doin' the Israelite

Exodus 11:2, 13:21, 14:27-28, 16:2-3,12, 17:2-4 (KJV)
Scriptural Reference on page 97

Have you ever thought after reading about,
How the Lord brought the Israelites out?
Just how they could murmur and complain,
It boggles my mind and spins my brain.

I call it, "Doin' the Israelite!"

I couldn't imagine after all God had done,
Wanting to turn back high-tail-it and run.
Back to bondage and the Pharaoh's whip,
And not wanting to make that glorious trip.

I call it, "Doin' the Israelite!"

After bringing them out with silver and gold,
Every man, woman, child from the young to the old.
After parting the sea and walking on dry land,
And destroying the enemy with a sweep of his hand.

I call it, "Doin' the Israelite!"

How could they slip back to their ungodly way,
While Moses was getting what God had to say
On the tablets of stone Gods' glorious Word,
Of which His people had never heard.

I call it, "Doin' the Israelite!"

Now remember how He led them by night and by day,
Leading them so evident all of the way.
And all of the miracles and the wondrous feats,
Water from stone and manna to eat.

I call it, "Doin' the Israelite!"

He kept them better than the birds or the lilies of the field,
It's hard to comprehend, it can't really be real,
But now as I take my wilderness walk,
Sometimes I have to check my thoughts and my talk.

Am I, "Doin' the Israelite?"

I find that, I too, murmur and complain,
And sometimes I think I'll go insane.
I know the Spirit of God dwells in me,
And I should walk by faith unable to see.

Am I, "Doin' the Israelite?"

It isn't as easy, as it looks,
I thought it would be, after reading His book.
His account of the Israelites warns all of us,
Of the possible fate if we doubt and mistrust.

Are you, "Doin' the Israelite?"

Saints, believe what I'm about to say,
You will do the Israelite every day.
Yes, I'm telling it right and telling it straight,
We are all filled, with fear, mistrust, and hate.

Are you, "Doin' the Israelite?"

Doin' the Israelite

Lord, help and forgive me, I repent and ask,
For strength and understanding, so I can last.
The entire way to the Promise land,
Don't leave me in the wilderness, bring me out by your hand.

I don't want to be caught, "Doin' the Israelite!"

Lord I want to be found steadfast and true,
Faithful to the end, believing in You.
You never said, it would be easy or a piece of cake,
But that tribulation would come, and it's for our sakes.

I'm growing in faith every day,
I believe you'll perfect me in every way.
But it's not because I am so good,
Or because I have faith like I should.

But because You are faithful and true to Your Word,
And what You have started, you'll finish, I've heard.
And in the end, everything will be right,
And I won't be caught, "Doin' the Israelite!"

Doin' the Israelite

Forgive or Forgive Not

Luke 6:37; Mark 11:25-26 (KJV)
Scriptural Reference on page 99

Forgive or forgive not, the choice is up to you.
But choose wisely and carefully whatever you do!

For to forgive not - can seal your very fate,
By eating you alive, with a cancer of consuming hate.

But to forgive - now you're talking my language here,
The sweetest of gestures, frees your Spirit, my dears!

Generations in You

Psalms 127:3-5, 128:3 (KJV)
Scriptural Reference on page 100

I have so many desires and dreams,
This life isn't long enough it seems.

For me to fulfill all that I want to do,
It's frustrating for me to attempt to.

But the Lord explained it to me just so,
So that I wouldn't get too anxious, you know.

That in all my dreams and desires,
Is just the vision of generations inspired.

The deeds of my children, grandchildren and more,
Lay in me, for I am just a door.

To the future of all that God has planned,
To accomplish through me by His loving hand.

So, don't regret what you didn't become,
It will happen in a grandchild, or daughter or son.

You didn't sacrifice your life in vain for the kids,
That famous painter, or athlete in future will live.

My soul is at peace,
My footsteps have been ordered by Him,
I look forward to the fulfillment in them.

All my dreams, I will fulfill through my seed,
This is God's amazing, fantastic plan indeed!

Dr. Lydia A. Woods

The Gift

Psalms 111:10; Proverbs 16:16-25 (KJV)
Scriptural Reference on page 101

Wisdom is the gift,
You want to give away,
But nobody seems to want it,
In this present day.

It's a valuable thing,
You'll pay a precious price,
It costs blood, sweat and tears,
And a piece of your life!

Not money, or silver,
Not even gold,
Can buy this precious thing,
Possessed by the old.

The old one wishes to make a gift,
To the young,
To friends and family,
To daughters and sons.

But no one seems,
To want to take it free,
They all choose to buy their own,
So let them be.

_-17-_

The Gift

Let them pay,
With their own blood, sweat, and tears,
For to pay for that thing,
Called wisdom could take years.

So, in buying your wisdom,
Buy this too,
That you can't give it to just anyone,
Only those who,

God sends to you,
Now you can give it away.
But hold tight,
To the wisdom until that day.

The giving is usually not to children,
Relatives, or friends
But a stranger who crosses your path,
Every now and then.

And with wisdom you'll begin,
To recognize,
Just who of those strangers,
Will cherish the prize!

The Gift

Go the Distance

Revelation 2:1-29, 3:1-22 (KJV)
Scriptural Reference on page 102

I like a good mystery,
I've read many in my time,
I work out the details
And plots in my mind.

Can't wait for the ending,
For the author to tell,
Just who is the bad guy
And who's going to jail!

Well, the Bible is the best mystery,
That I ever read,
It keeps me on edge,
So many plots in my head.

But I wouldn't get caught,
Not reading the end,
Cause to a mystery hound like me,
That's really an unforgivable sin.

So, it really amazes me,
How so many can resist,
Reading the last chapter,
And all that good ending miss.

Even the name of that chapter,
Rings quite true,
"Revelation" reveals the whole book,
To me and to you.

The author was clever,
For not all can see,
The final outcome,
Of this amazing mystery!

So, I'll reveal a little truth,
That few know,
Just what the overcomer receives,
When the distance they go.

For the race is not given,
To the swift or the strong,
But he that endures to the end,
Will never go wrong.

Now I found that the overcomer,
Will eat of the tree of life,
That tree in the garden,
Denied to Adam and his wife.

The overcomer will eat hidden manna,
Receive a stone of pure white,
A new name in that stone,
So John, the author, writes.

The overcomer gets power,
To rule over the nations,
Given by the Morning Star,
For the overcomer has learned His patience.

Go the Distance

White raiment is given ,
To show that we are pure,
Our name in the Book of Life,
Of that you can be sure.

Before the Father,
Our Savior confesses our name,
Also to the Angels in Heaven,
Our triumph proclaim.

A Pillar in the Temple of God,
We'll stand tall and straight,
Bearing the Name of our God,
And His city, I can hardly wait.

Our Lord's new name will be written,
On us for all to see,
Sealed there forever,
Unto all eternity.

So, go the distance,
And never faint or fear,
For your Salvation is at hand,
And Redemption is near.

Last, but not least,
The Lord has granted to thee,
To sit with Him in His throne,
Forever Saved and Free!

Dr. Lydia A. Woods

God's M.O.

1 Corinthians 1:26-27, 2:7, 3:19; Luke 2:7;Ephesians 3:5 (KJV)
Scriptural Reference on page 107

My relationship with the Father,
Is growing from day to day,
I'm learning of His unique character,
And a little something about His way.

How He doesn't come right at you,
He's not in your face plain and clear.
But you need to look a little deeper,
To see what's really going on here.

How he brought His Son in low estate,
Not a King upon a throne,
He is subtle and quite ingenious,
But if you're not careful you'll go wrong.

He takes the foolishness of man,
To confound the very wise,
Those discarded things of man,
Are the Lord's greatest prize.

The very thing that doesn't appeal to you,
And makes you want to run the other way,
Give it a second deeper look,
'Cause I discovered a secret one day.

God's M.O.

That Satan comes at you like an angel of light,
Disguising the bad behind the good,
And the minute you take the bait,
That's when he pulls the hood,

And uncovers the horrible mess,
That he has sucked you in for sure,
Now you're screaming for help,
Looking to God for the problem's cure.

So, don't be sucked in by outward appearances,
Listen carefully and look for God's M.O.
If it doesn't appeal to your flesh,
It's probably the way you ought to go.

So, when I am just plain obedient,
Even when I don't want to obey,
I'm always fantastically blessed,
When I give in and do it God's way.

God's M.O.

Dr. Lydia A. Woods

Good News

1 Corinthians 15:3, 15:52; Mark 13:24-27;
Revelation 1:7, 19:7-9; 20:1-3, 21:1-5 (KJV)
Scriptural Reference on page 108

Jesus died on the cross, for our souls,
He took our sickness in His body, so it was told.

That's how it all began a long time ago,
I'm not telling no tales that you don't know.

Brothers and sisters, you better listen up,
And take a long cool drink from the Jesus cup.

It's time we all got saved, in these terrible times,
You know the rapture's comin', don't be left behind.

He's comin' in the clouds, in a twinkle of an eye,
You know the Saints that are living, will not die.

So, believe in Him and in the power of His might,
'Cause He's coming like a thief, in the night.

And then there's seven long years, of hell on earth,
It's the tribulation times, Thank God for His Birth!

'Cause the Saints will be rockin' at the marriage feast,
And those here on earth will be fighting the beast.

Now He's coming back to set up His reign,
The earth will be changed, it won't be the same.

Good News

We're all coming back as Kings and Priest,
We won't have to contend with the beast.

He'll be sitting in the pit, with all of his gang,
Until Jesus is finished with His thousand-year reign.

Then Satan watch out cause yo' end is near,
The lake of fire is what you fear.

Now I'm telling the truth of what the scriptures say,
There's a Holy New Jerusalem on its way.

God will dwell with men on this new earth,
No sorrow will exist in this new birth.

So, get your heart right and set your mind,
And get Salvation now and put your sins behind.

I'm spreading the Good News throughout the Land,
That Jesus Christ, He is our man!
That Jesus Christ, He is our man!
That Jesus Christ, He is our man!

Good News

Dr. Lydia A. Woods

Has Done, Is Doing or Will Do

Psalms 71:15, 35:28, 40:5; Job 9:10 (KJV)
Scriptural Reference on page 110

I have a sister in the Lord,
That lives at a distance from me.
It's a long-distance call,
So I use nine cents a minute, 'cause it ain't free.

So, we can't call often,
And when we do there's quite a need,
For a Saint who knows the Word,
And has revelation on what they read.

And sometimes that need is just to report,
About what He has done, is doing or will do.
Now here's the thing that struck me the other day,
When the call was done, and we were through.

You know a strange thing seems to happen,
I've noticed every time, without fail,
That my feet no longer touch the ground,
And for the time being Satan is back in hell.

Just to talk about the Lord,
What He has done, is doing or will do,
Delights and thrills His soul,
And He takes pleasure in me and you.

And we are both edified and strengthened,
And ready to face the trials ahead.
Where two or more are gathered in His name,
Is much deeper than at first, I read.

There's a blessing to be found,
Just to speak about His Word,
What He has done, is doing or will do,
This is revelation I've never heard.

So, keep the conversation about others,
And negative things far from you,
Invest in bragging on the Lord,
What He has done, is doing or will do!

Has Done, Is Doing or Will Do

Dr. Lydia A. Woods

Holy Rollers

1 Peter 1:23, 2:9; John 1:12-13; 1 John 5:1 (KJV)
Scriptural Reference on page 111

In downtown Chicago,
On street corners you'll see,
Men ranting, repent,
Jesus loves you and me.

Quoting scriptures, dirty clothes,
Unshaven, not clean.
They make you think serving God,
Is a crazy man's thing.

It makes you afraid,
'Cause it's quite extreme.
To be avoided at all cost,
You know what I mean.

Then there are those,
We used to call "Holy Roller" types,
In church all day long,
And into the nights.

Every other word from their mouth,
Is, "Thank You Lord,"
And all they can talk about,
Is the Jesus they adore.

-29-

Holy Rollers

I never wanted those,
"Holy Rollers" to bother me,
'Cause they talked so strange,
I just wanted to flee!

But when I got saved,
A funny thing happened to me,
My eyes were opened,
And I began to see.

My ears could hear,
And I lost the fear,
And any testimony of the Lord,
And His Word I loved to hear.

And I'll talk about Him if you let me,
Night and day,
And I'll talk to anyone interested,
In what I have to say.

Now it has occurred to me,
What the Lord has secretly done.
One of those "Holy Rollers,"
I have without a doubt become!

Holy Rollers

How Many Times

Philippians 4:19 (KJV)
Scriptural Reference on page 112

How many times must I,
Snatch you from the jaws of the devourer,
For you to remember,
That I am there for you hour after hour.

How many times must I,
Meet your need,
For you to remember,
That you are my lamb that I will feed.

How many times must I,
Surprise you with the secrets of your heart,
For you to remember,
That it is sweet gifts to you that I wish to impart.

How many times must I,
Comfort you,
For you to remember,
That I will always be there to rescue.

How many times must I,
Bless your children,
For you to remember,
That I will carry your every burden.

How many times must I,
Put food on your table,
For you to remember,
That I will never forsake - I am more than able.

How many times must I,
Pay your bills,
For you to remember,
That to provide for you is my divine will.

How many times must I,
Keep you and your children in health,
For you to remember,
That My Son took your sickness onto Himself.

How many times before you will believe,
That I love you,
I will pursue you until you know,
That it is true.

Look back and count,
All that I have done,
I have blessed you so many times,
You can't remember everyone.

When revelation knowledge comes to you,
Of my endless love,
Then you can move from this grievous place,
And I'll lift you far above,

The day-to-day pressures of this world,
Filled with fear and strife,
And greater things I can accomplish,
Through your precious life.

How Many Times

So, remember when the enemy speaks to you,
Do what my Son taught you to,

Say, "It is written Satan, you have no power here".
Speak the Word with boldness and never fear,
That I will not honor my own Word when I hear.

How many times - they are endless, My Dear.

If Thou Be...

Luke 4:1-13 (KJV)
Scripture Reference on page 113

If thou be the Son of God,
Satan's question to Jesus -- Now that was odd!

Satan knew He was the only begotten Son,
Was he just fooling around, having a bit of fun?

Is Satan so stupid or something worse,
To expect Jesus to serve him and His Father curse?

Jesus came to do the Father's Will,
And Satan knew it -- so what's the deal?

Now I've always thought Satan, not to bright,
To question Jesus on the issue of His birthright,

And if he would question Jesus with so stupid a plan,
Then he'll put the question to any ordinary woman or man.

Yes, Satan questions our birthright day in and out,
Trying to cause confusion and set up doubt.

And his stupid plan has worked like a charm,
Saints are giving him power and being disarmed.

Questioning their birthright has caused many to doubt,
They have power to foil his plan and wipe him out.

Power given to them through the Holy Name,
Step up with faith and your birthright claim.

So that whosoever that believes in Him,
Can through faith in Jesus their Salvation win.

And when Satan questions -- If Thou Be ...
Say, it is written -- there is no doubt in me!

- Conversation with Ms. Serena Reese

If Thou Be...

If You Want to Make God Laugh!

Proverbs 19:21; Matthew 5:36; Isaiah 46:9-11 (KJV)
Scriptural Reference on page 114

The old folk used to say, "It's all in God's Hands,"
And if you want to make God laugh,
Just tell Him your plans!

That you're gonna do this and that,
You're over twenty-one and that's a fact,
You're big and bad, so much in control,
Do what you want 'cause you're grown and bold.

The world taught you well about the planning part,
Everybody does it, and that's being smart.
To become a responsible adult and grown,
You must get on the go, get a plan of your own.

The sooner you realize that you have no power,
To make things happen from hour to hour,
That you can't change one hair on your head,
That you didn't wake yourself up today to get out of bed.

If You Want to Make God Laugh!

That you're a little child who can't come in or go out,
It doesn't do any good to get mad or even pout.
Things are out of your control so get with the plan,
That everything is purposed by God's own hand.

You were bought with a price
Do you know just what that means?
You got to give it up,
No use making a childish scene.

Scripture says, "Many are the plans of a man,
But God's purposes will prevail throughout the land,"
Stop drowning in the sea of denial,
'Cause you're bound to Him all the while.

So, if you want to make God laugh today,
Just open your mouth, let Him hear you say,
That you've got plans and you're gonna do this and that,
Watch the Hand of God just slap you Back!

If You Want to Make God Laugh!

Dr. Lydia A. Woods

I'm Not Lucky – I'm Blessed!

Genesis 12:3, 26:4; Deuteronomy 7:3-14 (KJV)
Scriptural Reference on page 115

I tell people all the time,
I'm not lucky – I'm blessed.
Luck is a word the world uses,
But blessed is the term I prefer to confess.

Lucky is not in the vocabulary of God's Word,
Saints rid luck from your conversation today.
It's only God's grace and mercy,
That follows us as we journey in life's way.

Lucky is a term of Satan,
It involves witchcraft and chances of fate.
But promises of God's blessings to His children,
Is not magic, but a sure and solid mandate.

We live in the showering of His blessings,
We walk in grace and mercy from hour to hour,
Miracles are just everyday occurrences,
It's our birthright to live our lives in His power.

The power of His Word,
That transcends every wicked device,
There is power in our tongues,
Saints let's correct our speech, that's my advice.

Remember that it is not luck,
That comes and goes at Satan's whim,
But the state of our existence,
When we walk by Faith in Him.

In a Split Second

James 1:8; 2 Corinthians 10:5 (KJV)
Scriptural Reference on page 117

In a split second your mind,
Can conjure up disaster,
And your demise comes from,
The great deceiving master.

When trouble comes,
Your mind is as active as can be,
Ripe for the picking,
And panic sets in so thoroughly.

You have a vivid imagination,
That can lead you to the grave,
You worry and stress yourself out,
And then begin to behave,

Like a stressed-out nut,
Running here and running there,
Your weight goes up or down,
Then you begin to lose your hair.

You live and feed on fear,
And that's your daily bread,
It's amazing all the scenarios,
That you are playing out in your head.

If you look back and count,
What never came to be,
You will realize that the Word of God,
Can set you free.

Free from worry and stress,
And every evil work,
Free from your own thoughts,
That can drive you berserk.

Cast down those vain imaginings,
That come into your head,
Satan puts them there because,
He wants to see you dead.

So, stop this foolish worrying,
It will only shorten your life span,
Commit your future to the Lord,
Place yourself within His hand.

"Don't worry, be happy,"
As the songwriter* wrote one day,
Tell Satan to take a hike,
And pack his bags, be on his way.

In a Split Second

Dr. Lydia A. Woods

And in that split second,
When panic takes you to your doom,
Change your perspective, keep the faith,
For faith rids you of the gloom.

After you cast down those vain imaginings,
This is what you do,
Apply the Word of God, to your situation,
As you were commanded to.

Believe what the Word says,
It's not based on how good you are,
But on God's grace and mercy,
And his righteousness...By far!

* "Don't Worry, Be Happy." by Bobby McFerrin

Dr. Lydia A. Woods

It's Alright

James 1:5 (KJV)
Scriptural Reference on page 118

I'm like the kid who pesters their mother,
And my father and sisters and even my brother.
Wanting answers to every mysterious wonder,
So many questions – I like to ponder.

I want to know how a tree grows so high?
How many stars are in the sky?
How does a hummingbird really fly?
Mother, mother, please tell me why?

And with the Lord I am just the same,
I pray and pray and call His name.
Wanting answers to problems, clear vision, and sight,
But all He says, sometimes is, "It's Alright."

And when I get the "It's Alright," response, it's quite profound,
There is something inside me that settles down.
A peace that floods my very being,
I know the problem is solved without my seeing.

I'm coming to know the Father well,
And about Him to everyone I tell,
About His answers as we talk – that's quite,
Soothing to my Spirit each time I hear, "It's Alright."

It's Not About Money

Luke 12:22-34; Matthew 6:25-34 (KJV)
Scriptural Reference on page 119

Oh! I'm finally really getting it,
I'm kind of a slow learner you see,
It's not about having a lot of money,
But putting my trust in thee,

It rains on the just and unjust,
Equally rain falls into every life,
But it's how you deal with the problems,
How you handle the grief and the strife.

Now everyone is feeling the pressure,
Life is stressful, and everyone is running scared.
But do you have a place to run to,
When everyone else is losing their head?

I'm learning not to lose my cool,
When things seem to be going all astray,
It happens so often that I'm beginning to wonder,
Maybe this is just the norm for life today.

The Lord wants me to rely on Him,
Not on money to solve every ill,
It's not money I really need,
Because trust in the Lord is a better deal.

It's finally sinking into my thick skull,
The years of trial and tribulation is creating in me,
The ability to be lifted to a higher level,
Of Trust and Rest and Peace in thee.

It's Not About Money

It's War!

Ephesians 6:10-17 (KJV)
Scriptural Reference on page 121

It's War!
When you take Jesus and you're reborn,
There's something you should know, that's going on.

It's War!
In high places that you can't see,
Put on your Spiritual ears, and listen to me.

It's War!
Yeah, its war, that I'm talking about,
When I am finished there will be no doubt.

It's War!
Against darkness and wickedness on high,
If you listen well there's no fear you'll die!

It's War!
But the victory's yours, without a doubt,
Your Savior fought the fight and worked it all out.

It's War!
But there is a special way you fight,
You just stand still with all of your might.

It's War!
And there's a special armor you wear,
The helmet of Salvation won't muster your hair.

It's War!

And on your loins the Truth you'll wear,
The Breastplate of Righteousness won't even tear.

You have the Gospel of Peace upon your feet,
And with the Shield in hand you won't feel the heat,

From the wicked fiery darts being thrown at you,
You don't have to despair, you know what to do.

With the Sword in hand just lift it high,
And quench those darts and watch them fly.

But you're not hurt, you only have to stand,
And be very patient and wait on your Man.

Cause He's coming in a cloud to rescue you,
The Holy One of God, Tried and True.

It's War!
And you're commanded to watch and pray,
I can hear the Lord say on that final day,

Well done good soldier - come on in,
Did you have a doubt that we would win!

And in the end, you'll be proud to say,
I had my armor on and withstood the evil day.

It's War!

Dr. Lydia A. Woods

Joseph

Genesis 37:2-5, 9, 15, 31-35, 41:41-43, 45:1-5 (KJV)
Scriptural Reference on page 122

In the Bible there are people, whose stories are told,
I know you think they're outdated and very old.
But there's a lesson to learn for us today,
Let me lay it out in a simple way.

Now take Joseph for instance and what happened to him,
All those brothers who threw him over the rim,
Of that deep dark pit, then plotted his demise,
Joseph hadn't acted cool or very wise.

Jacob loved Joseph more than the others,
This caused a lot of hate in Joseph's brothers.
And beside all that, he made Joseph that coat,
It really made the brothers mad and got their goat.

But that's not all, there's a little more,
Joseph had those dreams, so the brothers evened the score.
Into slavery they sold him on that day,
Dipped the coat in blood and to Jacob did say,

That a wild beast had torn him from limb to limb,
Jacob mourned and grieved for his future was dim.
Cause his precious son was gone never to return,
He rent his clothes – His kin were very concerned.

-49-

Joseph

They could not comfort him, all the daughters and sons,
And that's how Joseph's long journey had begun.
Joseph went through trials and tribulations galore,
He was lied on, thrown in prison, I know his heart was sore.

He missed his father and even those brothers you see,
He had years to work out resentment, to set his soul free.
All through the bad times he held onto his God,
His masters thought him strange and very odd.

But God watched over Joseph for He had a plan,
To bring all Jacob's children to Goshen land.
Not only had Joseph changed, but the brothers too,
Joseph tested them; he gave them back their due.

They were repentive for the evil deed so long ago,
But God turned it to their good, don't you know.
For that's the secret I'm about to reveal to you,
There is one in every family that God works through.

For the salvation of the others, it's a glorious plan,
Are you the one that God has cut out with His hand?
Are you the odd one that never seems to fit in?
Hoping for salvation of all your family in the end?

Joseph

Calling on the name of the Lord every day,
On you wilderness walk, not seeing your way.
Well, take heart cause it's all promised to you,
God will hone His Word and see your family through.

Like Joseph He'll set you on high with His Son,
He'll raise you up after you have done.
You appointed tune in the wilderness,
As you cling to your God and sin resist.

See those stories aren't so old for us today,
Take heart and let them encourage you on your way!
Mary agreed as soon as she had heard,
"Be it unto me according to thy word."

Just Do It!

Mark 16:15-20 (KJV)
Scriptural Reference on page 125

These signs shall follow them that believe,
Come on Saints, I know that you can read.
I found these signs in Mark sixteen and seventeen,
I didn't read about this in any comic magazine!

It says, to use His name to cast the devil out,
Don't you think that's what Saints should be about?
Jesus cast the devil out while He walked among us,
We should use His name, not fear spirits, and trust.

That His Word is true, and there is power in His name.
Keep working that Word you won't be the same.
Now at first it might not look like you're doing a thing.
But in the spirit world you've created a scene.

You have rocked the house of where Satan lives.
Keep using the name until Satan gives.
Just keep it up and don't think to quit,
'Cause you're commanded to ...

"Just Do It!"

It also says, with new tongues they will speak,
So get your new tongue, get power, don't be weak.
Tongues edify you not anyone else, you see,
It's evidence of the Holy Spirit in thee.

It's a gift you ask for so make that choice,
Open up your mouth and give the Holy Spirit a voice.
Praying in the Spirit is a more perfect way,
To fulfill what He's commanded us to do every day.

It also builds that faith, and this pleases God,
I know it sounds kind of funny and you look odd.
But remember you're a peculiar people indeed.
Born of His Spirit a child of His seed.

Don't be concerned about how you look,
Cause it's written in His Holy Book.
Just keep it up and don't think to quit,
'Cause you're commanded to ...

"Just Do It!"

Just Do It!

It also says, to heal the sick,
Lay hands on them the healing is quick.
How many Saints have you seen doing this?
It doesn't take special gifts there is no risk.

They will talk about you, and probably laugh out loud,
While you are imitating the Son all the while.
Can you stand to look strange and face the doubt?
But remember that's what peculiar people are all about.

Now at first it might not look like you're doing a thing,
But in the spirit world you've created a scene.
You remind the devil that he can't stay,
He has to honor the Word and be on his way.

You have rocked the house of where Satan lives,
Keep using the name until Satan gives.
Just keep it up and don't think to quit,
Cause' you're commanded to …

"Just Do it!"

Dr. Lydia A. Woods

Just Give It!

Acts 20:35; Luke 6:34-38 (KJV)
Scriptural Reference on page 126

A borrower nor,
A lender be,
Just a giver,
'Cause it makes you free.

Free from violating,
Your Father's Word.
And honoring the teaching,
That you have heard.

There's bondage in borrowing,
From a friend.
Or a neighbor or bank,
And especially your kin.

Have you noticed that things tend,
To get in the way,
Trying to make it impossible,
For that debt to pay?

And when you are the lender,
Things are going on there,
Cause you're expecting your money back,
Just your fair share.

They said they would pay,
And you took it for true,
Now they can't be found –
Are they avoiding you?

Now resentment for that person,
Is building in your heart,
Because there was good and pure,
Intentions on your part.

Now there is a mess,
Between friends or your kin,
And both of you have fallen,
So easily into sin,

They had every intention,
Of paying it back,
Why does it always happen,
That they get sidetracked?

Now that's the wisdom,
In the Word you see,
And these kinds of problems,
Need never be.

Me mad at you,
And you resenting me,
Just give it!
Honor the Word, and be Free!

Just Give It!

Dr. Lydia A. Woods

Just Wait!

Psalms 25:3; 27:14; 37:18; Isaiah 40:31 (KJV)
Scriptural Reference on page 127

I'm tired Lord, I've had enough,
How many times must I learn this lesson of trust.
I learned to trust you when I had that trial,
I was praising Your Name all the while.

Didn't you see the way I handled myself,
I relied on You and trusted in Your wealth.
I lifted my hands and praised your name,
I worked the Word and drove Satan to shame.

So now that I learned that lesson you see,
I'm ready to move on – now go on and bless me!
Bless me with the riches and desires of my heart,
For Your Word promises me prosperity if I've done my part.

But Saints remember it's not you who decides,
When the lesson is learned and when you have arrived.
It's the Father who knows just when you are ready,
It takes many years to learn to trust and be steady.

Steady and sure, immovable, and steadfast,
Waiting on the Lord till you think you can't last.
And just when you think you can't go on,
You'll mount like an eagle and be airborne.

He'll give you strength to continue this race,
Because of His love and mercy and grace.
Be still, shut-up, it's not too late,
Learn to rest in Him and – Just Wait!

Just Wait!

Lean Not

Proverbs 3:5-6; James 1:5 (KJV)
Scriptural Reference on page 128

Lean not to thy own understanding,
For you haven't got all the facts.
Take it from the One who knows all,
For your understanding is feeble and lacks.

It lacks, the wisdom of the ages,
It lacks, because you're not full grown.
It lacks, because your wisdom is fuzzy.
It lacks, because of sin that is sown.

I know you made good grades in school.
You've always been told that you are smart.
But your intellect is no good in this realm,
In the Spirit it's faith that sets you apart.

So, take your understanding from the Father,
He is wise and has your best interest at heart,
He knows that you are a child just stumbling,
He is willing to pick you up and take your part.

So, lean not to thy own understanding,
Ask for wisdom, He will give it freely to you.
For His thoughts and His ways are much higher,
But it's His understanding that will see you through!

Lean Not

Dr. Lydia A. Woods

Master of Masters

*Matthew 4:1, 4:19, 5:1, 7:29, 8:26, 11:5; Luke 8:43-48;
John 2:1-11, 11:43-44 (KJV) Scriptural Reference on page 129*

The Master of Masters was a fisher of men,
He taught the people and forgave all their sin.
He was tempted of Satan in the wilderness,
But full of the Spirit He did resist.

He was pressed by the multitude from all around,
On the mountain He taught, and made the Word profound.
He delivered the sick from all their pain,
He broke down the law and made it plain.

He made the blind to see and He calmed the rain,
And healed the minds of those insane.
He turned the water to wine, at the wedding feast,
He sent foul, filthy spirits into the beast.

A woman with faith who believed in Him,
And did not believe her chances were dim.
Touched the hem of His garment and she got blessed,
And captured the virtue He did possess.

Now it's written all there in His Holy Book,
Just open it up and have a look.
He raised the dead to life, and made the lame to walk,
He spent time with His disciples, and they did talk.

About eternal life and the Father above,
And of that greatest commandment - How to Love.
He spoke in parables, so only they would know,
The ones with ears, could learn and grow,

Who open their hearts, and the Son accept,
And repent of their sins, which gives Him respect.
'Cause He's the Master of Masters, the Holy One,
The Alpha and Omega, God's Beloved Son.

Master of Masters

The Perfect Murder

Romans 7:14-21 (KJV)
Scriptural Reference on page 132

The perfect murder, I plot at night,
My enemy to put permanently out of sight!

It has ruined my life, so it must go,
I'm talking about my *Will* – you know.

I've tried to kill it many times before,
I've kicked it to the curb and out the door.

It won't stay dead or get in line.
But maybe it *Will* stay dead this time!

'Cause this time, I'm giving it up to the One,
Who's dealt with *Will* since times begun.

Since killing it is not the way,
I'll give it to God each and every day.

It's not killing that He has in mind,
But little adjustments made over time.

He's slowly lining it up with His own will,
'Cause a *Will* is something you just can't kill!

Resistance is Futile

1 Corinthians 6:17, 12:12-27 (KJV)
Scriptural Reference on page 133

Resistance is futile,
Trekkies know just what I mean.
The Borg is coming,
And it's a hopeless, frightening thing.

Wherever they go,
The purpose is clear.
To assimilate – and resistance,
Is futile, my dear.

Well, that was Hollywood's version,
Of the way it ought to be,
But if you understand the plot,
I know you will see.

That the Borg's plan isn't original,
They took their cue,
From the master planner,
Who is assimilating me and you.

Now if you resist – you remember,
The consequence of the Borg,
Either assimilate or be destroyed,
The choice is all yours.

Individual entities,
With one collective mind,
Working for an evil purpose,
To destroy all life forms and humankind.

Now the collective mind of God,
Is just the opposite you see,
To give eternal life to humankind,
And to set them forever free.

Free from evil, death and sin –
Please assimilate me now!
I will not put up a fight,
Because Resistance is Futile!

Seeds of Self-Destruction

James 1:26, 3:5-10; Proverbs 18:21, 25:23 (KJV)
Scriptural Reference on page 135

Seeds of self-destruction planted when we're young,
The tender, innocent child, unaware that it's begun.

If the seeds of self-destruction take root and have their way,
Satan's plan will be accomplished in us today!

Parents, relatives, and friends are the willing ones,
They do Satan's bidding with their wagging foolish tongues.

Instead of building you up, they speak about your lack,
Your precious sensitive feelings get trampled, just like that!

The cruelty of those words, the acts of unkind deeds,
They all contribute to the growing of self-destruction seeds.

By the time you become adult, the seed has blossomed into a tree,
And there is ugly hideous fruit, growing in you and me.

The seeds are various kinds - I'll name them for you,
There is self-doubt, self-hatred, self-frustration now you have a clue.

They produce low self-esteem, lack of confidence, and the like,
Changing our appearance to fit some standard to be right.

A standard that is self-destructive it denies just who you are,
You look into the mirror - you've turned into something quite bizarre!

If the seeds of self-destruction, go according to the plan,
Then Satan only has to wait for the destruction of man,

But God has a plan too, that calls you into His marvelous light,
A slow process begins that will put you back to right.

For what Satan meant for evil to destroy, steal, and kill,
We have a powerful weapon of defense – the human will.

And when we will to serve the Lord, we become new on the inside,
Those seeds of self-destruction can no longer in us abide.

The wicked plan has been overthrown; he is losing as I speak,
It sounded like a good one, but it was faulty and quite weak.

For no plan of self-destruction that Satan could ever think of,
Can stand against the forces of God's profound and precious love!

- Conversation with William C. Terry

Seeds of Self-Destruction

Simply Because You Are Mine

Matthew 7:11; 1 Corinthians 2:9-11; Isaiah 64:4;
Psalms 31:19 (KJV)
Scripture Reference on page 136

Have you ever been blessed by the Lord?

I have, so many times I can't even count.
And it was one day recently that I found out,
A mystery that was hidden from me,
I was blinded, and I didn't really see.

A truth that I had heard many times and should know,
That Jesus loves me, for the Bible tells me so,
But we only really know in part,
And can't truly understand until He expands our heart.

And it was on that day the Lord blessed me well,
My heart was full, and the tears began to swell.
He blessed me with the secrets of my Heart,
Only He and I knew about this part.

You see, I didn't have a revelation of the depth of His love,
And revelation knowledge comes from His Spirit above.

So, one day the Lord spoke softly to me,
"I don't bless you because you are so good,
Or because you always behave as you should,
I bless you because I am true and just and kind,
I bless you simply because you are mine."

So Be Like Job

Job 1:1, 8-12; 2:1-6; 42:12-13 (KJV)
Scriptural Reference on page 137

Job was a mighty man of God they say,
He made offerings to God, every day.

He was perfect, upright, and very devout,
And God told Satan, to check him out.

His animals and beasts were all carried away,
His servants were killed that terrible day.

A house it fell on his daughters and sons,
Only one was left, to tell all that was done.

Job ripped his clothes and was highly upset,
But he worshipped God, of that you can bet.

He blessed the name of the Lord and did not sin,
It sent Satan running back to the Lord again.

This time Satan set out to do bodily harm,
He thought his next plan would work like a charm.

Job was cursed with sore boils on that day,
But he blessed his God, any ol' way.

Now even Job's wife pressed him the most,
To curse his God, and give up the Ghost.

And even his friends tried to cause him to sin.
But he was full of the Spirit and he did win.

Cause the Latter End of Job was truly blessed,
For the faith and trust he did possess.

So be like Job in your steadfast Love,
And receive your blessings from God above.

(Rap Style)

So Be Like Job

Dr. Lydia A. Woods

So Great a Cloud of Witnesses

Hebrews 12:1 (KJV)
Scriptural Reference on page 139

Now that great cloud of witnesses,
Is watching as you run.
This race that's set before you,
Filled with hazards and hurdles,
Not quite my idea of fun.

I got a mental picture,
As I talked with a Saint the other day,
Of the size and number of the hurdles,
That we encounter along the way.

I was describing my life,
In racing terms of course,
I had just taken a big hurdle,
Caught my foot and hit the turf.

Now I'm lying on the track.
Scraped knees, bleeding hands, wounded pride,
And I look to the left,
As runners pass me right in stride.

I lay there for a moment,
Waiting for assistance from on High,
I'm moaning and groaning nursing my wounds,
And feeling like I might as well just die.

But death is not in the picture,
'Cause that's the easy way out.
I'm expected to pick myself up,
Take joy in my affliction, without doubt,

That I'm going to make it to the end,
Of this lifelong race that's set out for me.
Running hurdles in the dark,
With only faith to carry me.

But besides the faith to finish,
Just remember the league you're in,
For that Great Cloud of Witnesses,
Is cheering for your success to win.

And I heard that Cloud of Witnesses,
Just the other day.
As I pulled myself up from another fall,
And was stewing in my dismay.

That Cloud of Witnesses was great.
The number I couldn't quite make out.
And they were cheering rather loudly,
As if I was winning without a doubt.

So Great a Cloud of Witnesses

Dr. Lydia A. Woods

I realized at that moment,
That it didn't matter the shape I was in,
'Cause this race is not about strong or swift,
But enduring to the end.

Endurance isn't pretty,
Cause every mark has a tale to tell.
Of the battles with Satan,
In the very depths of hell.

But it's about the race,
And the cleansing process along the way.
So that we can stand without spot or blemish,
In His presence on that Day!

Dr. Lydia A. Woods

Somethin' Told Me

John 12:26; Ephesians 4:30; Luke 2:26 (KJV)
Scriptural Reference on page 140

Somethin' told me,
I should have turned left when I turned right,
Somethin' told me,
I should have called her late last night,

Somethin' told me,
Not to say those unkind words,
Somethin' told me,
That my bill was due on the third,

Somethin' told me,
That you were not doing so well,
Somethin' told me,
That I could get that dress at the mall on sale,

Somethin' told me,
Not to pick up that phone or go into that room,
Somethin' told me,
That he wasn't the right bridegroom.

If I had a dollar,
For all the times I've heard,
But did not heed the gentle voice,
Or the light, urging, words,

-77-

Somethin' Told Me

Of the faint and fleeting sound,
Within my being,
Somethin' told me,
Without my knowing or my seeing.

The Somethin' told me,
One day not long ago,
Will you stop saying,
"Somethin'" told you so and so.

My name is not "Somethin',"
Please call my name out right,
My name is Holy Spirit,
And I live within you out of sight.

I was sent by my Master,
To lead and guide you into truth,
My job is to protect you,
Bring you to remembrance. Do you need proof?

Just open up my Word,
And read about Me for yourself,
My name is not "Somethin',
"But I'm your Lord – It's Me Myself!

Somethin' Told Me

Take No Thought

Luke 12:22-30 (KJV)
Scriptural Reference on page 141

Take no thought – For what you should wear,
Take no thought – In this world of cares.

Take no thought – For your Father will provide.
If you'll only let Him – He will satisfy.

Take no thought – For where you should live.
Only learn that in any state you find yourself—Give!

Take no thought – For what you should eat,
For the Lord will supply your food, drink, and meat.

Take no thought – For any need,
For He is faithful to fulfill this promise indeed.

Take no thought – I know it's easy to say,
But if you will practice, it's the only way,

Take no thought – Means to renew that mind,
Every day to achieve perfection divine.

Take no thought – Is the ultimate tribute indeed,
For without *Faith* it's impossible to please.

Take no thought – Is the only way to live down here,
Free from worry, disappointment, frustration, and fear.

Take no thought, I'll say no more,
Just leave it all to the One we Adore!

There But For the Grace...

Luke 10:27-37; Matthew 22:39 (KJV)
Scriptural Reference on page 142

There but for the Grace of God - Go I,
These words I've often wondered why?

How can the murderer, prostitute, drunk be me!
Look deeper friend and you will see.

There but for the Grace - Go you or I,
And so you ask the question ... Why?

That same question asked to the Master long ago,
Who is my neighbor? - Explain it so...

That I may know just who they are,
Are they near or are they far.

Love your neighbor as yourself, the great command,
My neighbor *is* myself, now I understand.

The inner being created just like me,
No differences that I can see!

I could be them - But for the Grace,
I see myself within every face.

I look into the souls of men,
I see myself reflected within,

So, you are me and I am you,
From one God, one source, one family grew.

Compassion swells, I now know why,
There but for the Grace of God - Go I.

                    - Conversation with Mr. Gene Wideman

There But For the Grace...

True Way of Life

John 13:34-35, 14:6 (KJV)
Scriptural Reference on page 144

One day the Lord said to me,
When you think of Jesus what do you see?

I said, there is an image of a man in my mind,
Strong, gentle in spirit, loving and kind.

Then God said something that astonished me,
I'll forever change what you see.

He is not a man but something much more,
My Word will reveal what you missed before.

I am the Truth, the Way, and the Life, He said.
Ponder this a moment inside your head.

Now say it all together, God said to me
I am a true way of life – Now what do you see?

Not a man, but a plan – A concept big and vast,
This answers some of my questions at last.

I was blown away –
My understanding was opened that day.
I wanted to hear more of what the Lord had to say.

He opened my understanding the light was bright in my head,
It was hard to take in all that He said.

If Jesus is a true way of life, then this means,
There is only One Way to enter that door it seems.

That "True Way of Life" is simple to understand,
Love God with your whole self and your fellow man.

Then you have lived that true life indeed,
And there is evidence that you are His seed.

Then one can enter through the door if the life is pure,
Because you truly know Jesus and that's for sure.

It's not about what a mouth will say,
It's about the evidence in your life from day to day.

I am the Truth, the Way, and the Life – Live it and see,
Your life will tell if you really knew Me!

- Conversation with Bill, Keith, and Rick

True Way of Life

What's His Face?

Genesis 3:15; John 19:11 (KJV)
Scriptural Reference on page 145

A very long time ago, so the Bible tells,
A foul rotten thing in heaven did dwell.

He was cast from heaven on that fateful day,
He fell to earth, so the scriptures say.

And in his anger, he began to plot and plan,
To get revenge on God's beloved Man.

In the garden of Eden, he did beguile,
While deceiving Adam and Eve all the while.

Then Adam's power over the earth, he did take,
And from that day to this, war on man did make.

But almighty God was just a step ahead,
And sent His Word in the flesh, in man's stead.

In the flesh He came to save you and me,
They crucified Him so all could see.

And that's where the evil one made, his stupid mistake,
For the life of Jesus, he could not take.

'Cause no sin could be found in the Holy One,
The Lamb of God, His beloved Son.

That's when all of his power over you and me,
Was given back to our Savior, you see.

Now he walks around seeking to destroy,
Anyone who believes they are his toy.

But I'm, here to tell that no power exists
Over those who would only resist,

And claim Jesus as their Savior, the Holy One,
And believe in Him, their life has just begun.

So, put him under foot, when he talks to you,
'Cause you're the Righteousness of God, tried and true.

And he's a thief, a liar, and a big disgrace,
I can't remember his name, you know, "What's his face?"

What's His Face?

Dr. Lydia A. Woods

With His Own Blood

Acts 20:28; Hosea 2:19; Revelation 19:7-9, 21:9 (KJV)
Scriptural Reference on page 146

I love a love story,
As most women do.
Give me a happy ending,
Plus boxes of tissue too.

I'll cry you a bucket,
In the dark of any show.
'Cause a love story pulls,
At my heartstrings, anyway it goes.

Well, the greatest love story ever written,
I know of in this life,
Is the love of Jesus Christ for the church,
His sought-after wife.

The most romantic thing I know,
Is a man laying down His life,
For the woman that He loves,
For His precious, beloved wife.

The horrible death that He suffered,
So that His beloved could only live.
Is the most beautiful gift of love,
That anyone can give.

My favorite hymn ever,
I've loved it since a child.
The melody sweetly haunts me,
As I hum the tune awhile.

"From heaven He came and sought her,
To be His holy bride,
With His own blood He bought her,
And for her life He died.*"

But not like Romeo and Juliet,
Star-crossed lovers in that tale,
That only in death,
Can they together dwell.

Our love story is unsurpassed,
For not even death can hold,
This lover in the grave,
That's how this love story goes.

The ending tells,
Of the greatest victory won,
For God so loved the world,
He gave His only Son.

After giving up His life,
For His beloved precious Bride,
He is raised again to life,
And awaits her by His Side!

* "The Church's One Foundation" By Samuel J. Stone and Samuel S. Wesley

With His Own Blood

Dr. Lydia A. Woods

Scriptural References

Above All

John 14:13; 1 John 5:14; Ephesians 3:10 (KJV)

John 14:13 (KJV)
13 And whatsoever ye shall ask in my name, that will I do, that the Father may be glorified in the Son.

1 John 5:14 (KJV)
14 And this is the confidence that we have in him, that, if we ask any thing according to his will, he heareth us:

Ephesians 3:10 (KJV)
10 To the intent that now unto the principalities and powers in heavenly places might be known by the church the manifold wisdom of God,

Be Still!

Psalms 46:10 (KJV)

Psalms 46:10 (KJV)
10 Be still, and know that I am God: I will be exalted among the heathen, I will be exalted in the earth.

A Bible Character

Luke 22:47, 57, 60; 23:21-34; Mark 15:1, 10-11; 16:1; Matthew 21:24;
1 Peter 2:9 (KJV)

Luke 22:47 (KJV)
47 And while he yet spake, behold a multitude, and he that was called Judas, one of the twelve, went before them, and drew near unto Jesus to kiss him.

Luke 22:57 (KJV)
57 And he denied him, saying, Woman, I know him not.

Luke 22:60 (KJV)
60 And Peter said, Man, I know not what thou sayest. And immediately, while he yet spake, the cock crew.

Luke 23:21-34 (KJV)
21 But they cried, saying, Crucify him, crucify him.
22 And he said unto them the third time, Why, what evil hath he done? I have found no cause of death in him: I will therefore chastise him, and let him go.
23 And they were instant with loud voices, requiring that he might be crucified. And the voices of them and of the chief priests prevailed.
24 And Pilate gave sentence that it should be as they required.
25 And he released unto them him that for sedition and murder was cast into prison, whom they had desired; but he delivered Jesus to their will.
26 And as they led him away, they laid hold upon one Simon, a Cyrenian, coming out of the country, and on him they laid the cross, that he might bear it after Jesus.
27 And there followed him a great company of people, and of women, which also bewailed and lamented him.
28 But Jesus turning unto them said, Daughters of Jerusalem, weep not for me, but weep for yourselves, and for your children.

29 For, behold, the days are coming, in the which they shall say, Blessed are the barren, and the wombs that never bare, and the paps which never gave suck.

30 Then shall they begin to say to the mountains, Fall on us; and to the hills, Cover us.

31 For if they do these things in a green tree, what shall be done in the dry?

32 And there were also two other, malefactors, led with him to be put to death.

33 And when they were come to the place, which is called Calvary, there they crucified him, and the malefactors, one on the right hand, and the other on the left.

34 Then said Jesus, Father, forgive them; for they know not what they do. And they parted his raiment, and cast lots.

Mark 15:1 (KJV)
1 And straightway in the morning the chief priests held a consultation with the elders and scribes and the whole council, and bound Jesus, and carried him away, and delivered him to Pilate.

Mark 15:10-11 (KJV)
10 For he knew that the chief priests had delivered him for envy.
11 But the chief priests moved the people, that he should rather release Barabbas unto them.

Mark 16:1 (KJV)
1 And when the sabbath was past, Mary Magdalene, and Mary the mother of James, and Salome, had bought sweet spices, that they might come and anoint him.

Matthew 21:24 (KJV)
24 And Jesus answered and said unto them, I also will ask you one thing, which if ye tell me, I in like wise will tell you by what authority I do these things.

1 Peter 2:9 (KJV)
9 But ye are a chosen generation, a royal priesthood, an holy nation, a peculiar people; that ye should shew forth the praises of him who hath called you out of darkness into his marvellous light;

Dr. Lydia A. Woods

A Blessing – Not a Curse!

Psalms 127:3-5 (KJV)

Psalms 127:3-5 (KJV)

3 Lo, children are an heritage of the Lord: and the fruit of the womb is his reward.

4 As arrows are in the hand of a mighty man; so are children of the youth.

5 Happy is the man that hath his quiver full of them: they shall not be ashamed, but they shall speak with the enemies in the gate.

But For Your Praying Saints

Ephesians 6:18; 1 Thessalonians 5:17; James 5:16 (KJV)

Ephesians 6:18 (KJV)

[18] Praying always with all prayer and supplication in the Spirit, and watching thereunto with all perseverance and supplication for all saints;

1 Thessalonians 5:17 (KJV)

[17] Pray without ceasing.

James 5:16 (KJV)

[16] Confess your faults one to another, and pray one for another, that ye may be healed. The effectual fervent prayer of a righteous man availeth much.

Doin' the Israelite

Exodus 11:2; 13:21; 14:27-28; 16:2-3,12; 17:2-4 (KJV)

Exodus 11:2 (KJV)

2 Speak now in the ears of the people, and let every man borrow of his neighbour, and every woman of her neighbour, jewels of silver and jewels of gold.

Exodus 13:21 (KJV)

21 And the Lord went before them by day in a pillar of a cloud, to lead them the way; and by night in a pillar of fire, to give them light; to go by day and night:

Exodus 14:27-28 (KJV)

27 And Moses stretched forth his hand over the sea, and the sea returned to his strength when the morning appeared; and the Egyptians fled against it; and the Lord overthrew the Egyptians in the midst of the sea.
28 And the waters returned, and covered the chariots, and the horsemen, and all the host of Pharaoh that came into the sea after them; there remained not so much as one of them.

Exodus 16:2-3 (KJV)

2 And the whole congregation of the children of Israel murmured against Moses and Aaron in the wilderness:
3 And the children of Israel said unto them, Would to God we had died by the hand of the Lord in the land of Egypt, when we sat by the flesh pots, and when we did eat bread to the full; for ye have brought us forth into this wilderness, to kill this whole assembly with hunger.

Exodus 16:12 (KJV)

12 I have heard the murmurings of the children of Israel: speak unto them, saying, At even ye shall eat flesh, and in the morning ye shall be filled with bread; and ye shall know that I am the Lord your God.

Exodus 17:2-4 (KJV)

2 Wherefore the people did chide with Moses, and said, Give us water that we may drink. And Moses said unto them, Why chide ye with me? wherefore do ye tempt the Lord?

3 And the people thirsted there for water; and the people murmured against Moses, and said, Wherefore is this that thou hast brought us up out of Egypt, to kill us and our children and our cattle with thirst?

4 And Moses cried unto the Lord, saying, What shall I do unto this people? they be almost ready to stone me.

Forgive or Forgive Not

Luke 6:37; Mark 11:25-26 (KJV)

Luke 6:37 (KJV)

37 Judge not, and ye shall not be judged: condemn not, and ye shall not be condemned: forgive, and ye shall be forgiven:

Mark 11:25-26 (KJV)

25 And when ye stand praying, forgive, if ye have ought against any: that your Father also which is in heaven may forgive you your trespasses.
26 But if ye do not forgive, neither will your Father which is in heaven forgive your trespasses.

Generations in You

Psalms 127:3-5, 128:3 (KJV)

Psalms 127:3-5 (KJV)
[3] Lo, children are an heritage of the Lord: and the fruit of the womb is his reward.
[4] As arrows are in the hand of a mighty man; so are children of the youth.
[5] Happy is the man that hath his quiver full of them: they shall not be ashamed, but they shall speak with the enemies in the gate.

Psalms 128:3 (KJV)
[3] Thy wife shall be as a fruitful vine by the sides of thine house: thy children like olive plants round about thy table.

The Gift

Psalms 111:10; Proverbs 16:16-25 (KJV)

Psalms 111:10 (KJV)

10 The fear of the Lord is the beginning of wisdom: a good understanding have all they that do his commandments: his praise endureth for ever.

Proverbs 16:16-25 (KJV)

16 How much better is it to get wisdom than gold! and to get understanding rather to be chosen than silver!

17 The highway of the upright is to depart from evil: he that keepeth his way preserveth his soul.

18 Pride goeth before destruction, and an haughty spirit before a fall.

19 Better it is to be of an humble spirit with the lowly, than to divide the spoil with the proud.

20 He that handleth a matter wisely shall find good: and whoso trusteth in the Lord, happy is he.

21 The wise in heart shall be called prudent: and the sweetness of the lips increaseth learning.

22 Understanding is a wellspring of life unto him that hath it: but the instruction of fools is folly.

23 The heart of the wise teacheth his mouth, and addeth learning to his lips.

24 Pleasant words are as an honeycomb, sweet to the soul, and health to the bones.

25 There is a way that seemeth right unto a man, but the end thereof are the ways of death.

Go the Distance

Revelation 2:1-29, 3:1-22 (KJV)

Revelation 2:1-29 (KJV)

[1] Unto the angel of the church of Ephesus write; These things saith he that holdeth the seven stars in his right hand, who walketh in the midst of the seven golden candlesticks;

[2] I know thy works, and thy labour, and thy patience, and how thou canst not bear them which are evil: and thou hast tried them which say they are apostles, and are not, and hast found them liars:

[3] And hast borne, and hast patience, and for my name's sake hast laboured, and hast not fainted.

[4] Nevertheless I have somewhat against thee, because thou hast left thy first love.

[5] Remember therefore from whence thou art fallen, and repent, and do the first works; or else I will come unto thee quickly, and will remove thy candlestick out of his place, except thou repent.

[6] But this thou hast, that thou hatest the deeds of the Nicolaitanes, which I also hate.

[7] He that hath an ear, let him hear what the Spirit saith unto the churches; To him that overcometh will I give to eat of the tree of life, which is in the midst of the paradise of God.

[8] And unto the angel of the church in Smyrna write; These things saith the first and the last, which was dead, and is alive;

[9] I know thy works, and tribulation, and poverty, (but thou art rich) and I know the blasphemy of them which say they are Jews, and are not, but are the synagogue of Satan.

[10] Fear none of those things which thou shalt suffer: behold, the devil shall cast some of you into prison, that ye may be tried; and ye shall have tribulation ten days: be thou faithful unto death, and I will give thee a crown of life.

[11] He that hath an ear, let him hear what the Spirit saith unto the churches; He that overcometh shall not be hurt of the second death.

[12] And to the angel of the church in Pergamos write; These things saith he which hath the sharp sword with two edges;

[13] I know thy works, and where thou dwellest, even where Satan's seat is: and thou holdest fast my name, and hast not denied my faith, even in those days wherein Antipas was my faithful martyr, who was slain among you, where Satan dwelleth.

[14] But I have a few things against thee, because thou hast there them that hold the doctrine of Balaam, who taught Balac to cast a stumblingblock before the children of Israel, to eat things sacrificed unto idols, and to commit fornication.

[15] So hast thou also them that hold the doctrine of the Nicolaitanes, which thing I hate.

[16] Repent; or else I will come unto thee quickly, and will fight against them with the sword of my mouth.

[17] He that hath an ear, let him hear what the Spirit saith unto the churches; To him that overcometh will I give to eat of the hidden manna, and will give him a white stone, and in the stone a new name written, which no man knoweth saving he that receiveth it.

[18] And unto the angel of the church in Thyatira write; These things saith the Son of God, who hath his eyes like unto a flame of fire, and his feet are like fine brass;

[19] I know thy works, and charity, and service, and faith, and thy patience, and thy works; and the last to be more than the first.

[20] Notwithstanding I have a few things against thee, because thou sufferest that woman Jezebel, which calleth herself a prophetess, to teach and to seduce my servants to commit fornication, and to eat things sacrificed unto idols.

[21] And I gave her space to repent of her fornication; and she repented not.

[22] Behold, I will cast her into a bed, and them that commit adultery with her into great tribulation, except they repent of their deeds.

²³ And I will kill her children with death; and all the churches shall know that I am he which searcheth the reins and hearts: and I will give unto every one of you according to your works.

²⁴ But unto you I say, and unto the rest in Thyatira, as many as have not this doctrine, and which have not known the depths of Satan, as they speak; I will put upon you none other burden.

²⁵ But that which ye have already hold fast till I come.

²⁶ And he that overcometh, and keepeth my works unto the end, to him will I give power over the nations:

²⁷ And he shall rule them with a rod of iron; as the vessels of a potter shall they be broken to shivers: even as I received of my Father.

²⁸ And I will give him the morning star.

²⁹ He that hath an ear, let him hear what the Spirit saith unto the churches.

Revelation 3:1-22 (KJV)

¹ And unto the angel of the church in Sardis write; These things saith he that hath the seven Spirits of God, and the seven stars; I know thy works, that thou hast a name that thou livest, and art dead.

² Be watchful, and strengthen the things which remain, that are ready to die: for I have not found thy works perfect before God.

³ Remember therefore how thou hast received and heard, and hold fast, and repent. If therefore thou shalt not watch, I will come on thee as a thief, and thou shalt not know what hour I will come upon thee.

⁴ Thou hast a few names even in Sardis which have not defiled their garments; and they shall walk with me in white: for they are worthy.

⁵ He that overcometh, the same shall be clothed in white raiment; and I will not blot out his name out of the book of life, but I will confess his name before my Father, and before his angels.

6 He that hath an ear, let him hear what the Spirit saith unto the churches.

7 And to the angel of the church in Philadelphia write; These things saith he that is holy, he that is true, he that hath the key of David, he that openeth, and no man shutteth; and shutteth, and no man openeth;

8 I know thy works: behold, I have set before thee an open door, and no man can shut it: for thou hast a little strength, and hast kept my word, and hast not denied my name.

9 Behold, I will make them of the synagogue of Satan, which say they are Jews, and are not, but do lie; behold, I will make them to come and worship before thy feet, and to know that I have loved thee.

10 Because thou hast kept the word of my patience, I also will keep thee from the hour of temptation, which shall come upon all the world, to try them that dwell upon the earth.

11 Behold, I come quickly: hold that fast which thou hast, that no man take thy crown.

12 Him that overcometh will I make a pillar in the temple of my God, and he shall go no more out: and I will write upon him the name of my God, and the name of the city of my God, which is new Jerusalem, which cometh down out of heaven from my God: and I will write upon him my new name.

13 He that hath an ear, let him hear what the Spirit saith unto the churches.

14 And unto the angel of the church of the Laodiceans write; These things saith the Amen, the faithful and true witness, the beginning of the creation of God;

15 I know thy works, that thou art neither cold nor hot: I would thou wert cold or hot.

16 So then because thou art lukewarm, and neither cold nor hot, I will spue thee out of my mouth.

Scripture References   Go the Distance

¹⁷ Because thou sayest, I am rich, and increased with goods, and have need of nothing; and knowest not that thou art wretched, and miserable, and poor, and blind, and naked:

¹⁸ I counsel thee to buy of me gold tried in the fire, that thou mayest be rich; and white raiment, that thou mayest be clothed, and that the shame of thy nakedness do not appear; and anoint thine eyes with eyesalve, that thou mayest see.

¹⁹ As many as I love, I rebuke and chasten: be zealous therefore, and repent.

²⁰ Behold, I stand at the door, and knock: if any man hear my voice, and open the door, I will come in to him, and will sup with him, and he with me.

²¹ To him that overcometh will I grant to sit with me in my throne, even as I also overcame, and am set down with my Father in his throne.

²² He that hath an ear, let him hear what the Spirit saith unto the churches.

God's M.O.

1 Corinthians 1:26-27, 2:7, 3:19; Luke 2:7; Ephesians 3:5 (KJV)

1 Corinthians 1:26-27 (KJV)

26 For ye see your calling, brethren, how that not many wise men after the flesh, not many mighty, not many noble, are called:

27 But God hath chosen the foolish things of the world to confound the wise; and God hath chosen the weak things of the world to confound the things which are mighty;

1 Corinthians 2:7 (KJV)

7 But we speak the wisdom of God in a mystery, even the hidden wisdom, which God ordained before the world unto our glory:

1 Corinthians 3:19 (KJV)

19 For the wisdom of this world is foolishness with God. For it is written, He taketh the wise in their own craftiness.

Luke 2:7 (KJV)

7 And she brought forth her firstborn son, and wrapped him in swaddling clothes, and laid him in a manger; because there was no room for them in the inn.

Ephesians 3:5 (KJV)

5 Which in other ages was not made known unto the sons of men, as it is now revealed unto his holy apostles and prophets by the Spirit;

Good News

1 Corinthians 15:3, 15:52; Mark 13:24-27; Revelation 1:7, 19:7-9, 20:1-3, 21:1-5 (KJV)

1 Corinthians 15:3 (KJV)

3 For I delivered unto you first of all that which I also received, how that Christ died for our sins according to the scriptures;

1 Corinthians 15:52 (KJV)

52 In a moment, in the twinkling of an eye, at the last trump: for the trumpet shall sound, and the dead shall be raised incorruptible, and we shall be changed.

Mark 13:24-27 (KJV)

24 But in those days, after that tribulation, the sun shall be darkened, and the moon shall not give her light,
25 And the stars of heaven shall fall, and the powers that are in heaven shall be shaken.
26 And then shall they see the Son of man coming in the clouds with great power and glory.
27 And then shall he send his angels, and shall gather together his elect from the four winds, from the uttermost part of the earth to the uttermost part of heaven.

Revelation 1:7 (KJV)

7 Behold, he cometh with clouds; and every eye shall see him, and they also which pierced him: and all kindreds of the earth shall wail because of him. Even so, Amen.

Revelation 19:7-9 (KJV)

7 Let us be glad and rejoice, and give honour to him: for the marriage of the Lamb is come, and his wife hath made herself ready.
8 And to her was granted that she should be arrayed in fine linen, clean and white: for the fine linen is the righteousness of saints.

9 And he saith unto me, Write, Blessed are they which are called unto the marriage supper of the Lamb. And he saith unto me, These are the true sayings of God.

Revelation 20:1-3 (KJV)
1 And I saw an angel come down from heaven, having the key of the bottomless pit and a great chain in his hand.
2 And he laid hold on the dragon, that old serpent, which is the Devil, and Satan, and bound him a thousand years,
3 And cast him into the bottomless pit, and shut him up, and set a seal upon him, that he should deceive the nations no more, till the thousand years should be fulfilled: and after that he must be loosed a little season.

Revelation 21:1-5 (KJV)
1 And I saw a new heaven and a new earth: for the first heaven and the first earth were passed away; and there was no more sea.
2 And I John saw the holy city, new Jerusalem, coming down from God out of heaven, prepared as a bride adorned for her husband.
3 And I heard a great voice out of heaven saying, Behold, the tabernacle of God is with men, and he will dwell with them, and they shall be his people, and God himself shall be with them, and be their God.
4 And God shall wipe away all tears from their eyes; and there shall be no more death, neither sorrow, nor crying, neither shall there be any more pain: for the former things are passed away.
5 And he that sat upon the throne said, Behold, I make all things new. And he said unto me, Write: for these words are true and faithful.

Has Done, Is Doing or Will Do

Psalms 35:28, 40:5, 71:15, Job 9:10 (KJV)

Psalms 35:28 (KJV)
28 And my tongue shall speak of thy righteousness and of thy praise all the day long.

Psalms 40:5 (KJV)
5 Many, O Lord my God, are thy wonderful works which thou hast done, and thy thoughts which are to us-ward: they cannot be reckoned up in order unto thee: if I would declare and speak of them, they are more than can be numbered.

Psalms 71:15 (KJV)
15 My mouth shall shew forth thy righteousness and thy salvation all the day; for I know not the numbers thereof.

Job 9:10 (KJV)
10 Which doeth great things past finding out; yea, and wonders without number.

Holy Rollers

1 Peter 1:23, 2:9; John 1:12-13; 1 John 5:1 (KJV)

1 Peter 1:23 (KJV)
23 Being born again, not of corruptible seed, but of incorruptible, by the word of God, which liveth and abideth for ever.

1 Peter 2:9 (KJV)
9 But ye are a chosen generation, a royal priesthood, an holy nation, a peculiar people; that ye should shew forth the praises of him who hath called you out of darkness into his marvellous light;

John 1:12-13 (KJV)
12 But as many as received him, to them gave he power to become the sons of God, even to them that believe on his name:
13 Which were born, not of blood, nor of the will of the flesh, nor of the will of man, but of God.

1 John 5:1 (KJV)
1 Whosoever believeth that Jesus is the Christ is born of God: and every one that loveth him that begat loveth him also that is begotten of him.

How Many Times

Philippians 4:19 (KJV)

Philippians 4:19 (KJV)
19 But my God shall supply all your need according to his riches in glory by Christ Jesus.

If Thou Be...

Luke 4:1-13 (KJV)

Luke 4:1-13 (KJV)

[1] And Jesus being full of the Holy Ghost returned from Jordan, and was led by the Spirit into the wilderness,

[2] Being forty days tempted of the devil. And in those days he did eat nothing: and when they were ended, he afterward hungered.

[3] And the devil said unto him, If thou be the Son of God, command this stone that it be made bread.

[4] And Jesus answered him, saying, It is written, That man shall not live by bread alone, but by every word of God.

[5] And the devil, taking him up into an high mountain, shewed unto him all the kingdoms of the world in a moment of time.

[6] And the devil said unto him, All this power will I give thee, and the glory of them: for that is delivered unto me; and to whomsoever I will I give it.

[7] If thou therefore wilt worship me, all shall be thine.

[8] And Jesus answered and said unto him, Get thee behind me, Satan: for it is written, Thou shalt worship the Lord thy God, and him only shalt thou serve.

[9] And he brought him to Jerusalem, and set him on a pinnacle of the temple, and said unto him, If thou be the Son of God, cast thyself down from hence:

[10] For it is written, He shall give his angels charge over thee, to keep thee:

[11] And in their hands they shall bear thee up, lest at any time thou dash thy foot against a stone.

[12] And Jesus answering said unto him, It is said, Thou shalt not tempt the Lord thy God.

[13] And when the devil had ended all the temptation, he departed from him for a season.

If You Want to Make God Laugh!

Proverbs 19:21; Matthew 5:36; Isaiah 46:9-11 (KJV)

Proverbs 19:21 (KJV)

[21] There are many devices in a man's heart; nevertheless the counsel of the Lord, that shall stand.

Matthew 5:36 (KJV)

[36] Neither shalt thou swear by thy head, because thou canst not make one hair white or black.

Isaiah 46:9-11 (KJV)

[9] Remember the former things of old: for I am God, and there is none else; I am God, and there is none like me,

[10] Declaring the end from the beginning, and from ancient times the things that are not yet done, saying, My counsel shall stand, and I will do all my pleasure:

[11] Calling a ravenous bird from the east, the man that executeth my counsel from a far country: yea, I have spoken it, I will also bring it to pass; I have purposed it, I will also do it.

Dr. Lydia A. Woods

I'm Not Lucky - I'm Blessed!

Genesis 12:3, 26:4; Deuteronomy 7:3-14 (KJV)

Genesis 12:3 (KJV)
3 And I will bless them that bless thee, and curse him that curseth thee: and in thee shall all families of the earth be blessed.

Genesis 26:4 (KJV)
4 And I will make thy seed to multiply as the stars of heaven, and will give unto thy seed all these countries; and in thy seed shall all the nations of the earth be blessed;

Deuteronomy 7:3-14 (KJV)
3 Neither shalt thou make marriages with them; thy daughter thou shalt not give unto his son, nor his daughter shalt thou take unto thy son.
4 For they will turn away thy son from following me, that they may serve other gods: so will the anger of the Lord be kindled against you, and destroy thee suddenly.
5 But thus shall ye deal with them; ye shall destroy their altars, and break down their images, and cut down their groves, and burn their graven images with fire.
6 For thou art an holy people unto the Lord thy God: the Lord thy God hath chosen thee to be a special people unto himself, above all people that are upon the face of the earth.
7 The Lord did not set his love upon you, nor choose you, because ye were more in number than any people; for ye were the fewest of all people:
8 But because the Lord loved you, and because he would keep the oath which he had sworn unto your fathers, hath the Lord brought you out with a mighty hand, and redeemed you out of the house of bondmen, from the hand of Pharaoh king of Egypt.

-115-
Scripture References   I'm Not Lucky – I'm Blessed!

9 Know therefore that the Lord thy God, he is God, the faithful God, which keepeth covenant and mercy with them that love him and keep his commandments to a thousand generations;

10 And repayeth them that hate him to their face, to destroy them: he will not be slack to him that hateth him, he will repay him to his face.

11 Thou shalt therefore keep the commandments, and the statutes, and the judgments, which I command thee this day, to do them.

12 Wherefore it shall come to pass, if ye hearken to these judgments, and keep, and do them, that the Lord thy God shall keep unto thee the covenant and the mercy which he sware unto thy fathers:

13 And he will love thee, and bless thee, and multiply thee: he will also bless the fruit of thy womb, and the fruit of thy land, thy corn, and thy wine, and thine oil, the increase of thy kine, and the flocks of thy sheep, in the land which he sware unto thy fathers to give thee.

14 Thou shalt be blessed above all people: there shall not be male or female barren among you, or among your cattle.

In a Split Second

James 1:8; 2 Corinthians 10:5 (KJV)

James 1:8 (KJV)

[8] A double minded man is unstable in all his ways.

2 Corinthians 10:5 (KJV)

[5] Casting down imaginations, and every high thing that exalteth itself against the knowledge of God, and bringing into captivity every thought to the obedience of Christ;

It's Alright

James 1:5 (KJV)

James 1:5 (KJV)
[5] If any of you lack wisdom, let him ask of God, that giveth to all men liberally, and upbraideth not; and it shall be given him.

Dr. Lydia A. Woods

It's Not About Money

Luke 12:22-34; Matthew 6:25-34 (KJV)

Luke 12:22-34 (KJV)

22 And he said unto his disciples, Therefore I say unto you, Take no thought for your life, what ye shall eat; neither for the body, what ye shall put on.

23 The life is more than meat, and the body is more than raiment.

24 Consider the ravens: for they neither sow nor reap; which neither have storehouse nor barn; and God feedeth them: how much more are ye better than the fowls?

25 And which of you with taking thought can add to his stature one cubit?

26 If ye then be not able to do that thing which is least, why take ye thought for the rest?

27 Consider the lilies how they grow: they toil not, they spin not; and yet I say unto you, that Solomon in all his glory was not arrayed like one of these.

28 If then God so clothe the grass, which is to day in the field, and to morrow is cast into the oven; how much more will he clothe you, O ye of little faith?

29 And seek not ye what ye shall eat, or what ye shall drink, neither be ye of doubtful mind.

30 For all these things do the nations of the world seek after: and your Father knoweth that ye have need of these things.

31 But rather seek ye the kingdom of God; and all these things shall be added unto you.

32 Fear not, little flock; for it is your Father's good pleasure to give you the kingdom.

33 Sell that ye have, and give alms; provide yourselves bags which wax not old, a treasure in the heavens that faileth not, where no thief approacheth, neither moth corrupteth.

34 For where your treasure is, there will your heart be also.

-119-

Matthew 6:25-34 (KJV)

[25] Therefore I say unto you, Take no thought for your life, what ye shall eat, or what ye shall drink; nor yet for your body, what ye shall put on. Is not the life more than meat, and the body than raiment?

[26] Behold the fowls of the air: for they sow not, neither do they reap, nor gather into barns; yet your heavenly Father feedeth them. Are ye not much better than they?

[27] Which of you by taking thought can add one cubit unto his stature?

[28] And why take ye thought for raiment? Consider the lilies of the field, how they grow; they toil not, neither do they spin:

[29] And yet I say unto you, That even Solomon in all his glory was not arrayed like one of these.

[30] Wherefore, if God so clothe the grass of the field, which to day is, and to morrow is cast into the oven, shall he not much more clothe you, O ye of little faith?

[31] Therefore take no thought, saying, What shall we eat? or, What shall we drink? or, Wherewithal shall we be clothed?

[32] (For after all these things do the Gentiles seek:) for your heavenly Father knoweth that ye have need of all these things.

[33] But seek ye first the kingdom of God, and his righteousness; and all these things shall be added unto you.

[34] Take therefore no thought for the morrow: for the morrow shall take thought for the things of itself. Sufficient unto the day is the evil thereof.

Dr. Lydia A. Woods

It's War!

Ephesians 6:10-17 (KJV)

Ephesians 6:10-17 (KJV)

[10] Finally, my brethren, be strong in the Lord, and in the power of his might.

[11] Put on the whole armour of God, that ye may be able to stand against the wiles of the devil.

[12] For we wrestle not against flesh and blood, but against principalities, against powers, against the rulers of the darkness of this world, against spiritual wickedness in high places.

[13] Wherefore take unto you the whole armour of God, that ye may be able to withstand in the evil day, and having done all, to stand.

[14] Stand therefore, having your loins girt about with truth, and having on the breastplate of righteousness;

[15] And your feet shod with the preparation of the gospel of peace;

[16] Above all, taking the shield of faith, wherewith ye shall be able to quench all the fiery darts of the wicked.

[17] And take the helmet of salvation, and the sword of the Spirit, which is the word of God:

Joseph

Genesis 37:2-5, 9, 15, 31-35; 41:41-43, 45:1-5 (KJV)

Genesis 37:2-5 (KJV)
2 These are the generations of Jacob. Joseph, being seventeen years old, was feeding the flock with his brethren; and the lad was with the sons of Bilhah, and with the sons of Zilpah, his father's wives: and Joseph brought unto his father their evil report.
3 Now Israel loved Joseph more than all his children, because he was the son of his old age: and he made him a coat of many colours.
4 And when his brethren saw that their father loved him more than all his brethren, they hated him, and could not speak peaceably unto him.
5 And Joseph dreamed a dream, and he told it his brethren: and they hated him yet the more.

Genesis 37:9 (KJV)
9 And he dreamed yet another dream, and told it his brethren, and said, Behold, I have dreamed a dream more; and, behold, the sun and the moon and the eleven stars made obeisance to me.

Genesis 37:15 (KJV)
15 And a certain man found him, and, behold, he was wandering in the field: and the man asked him, saying, What seekest thou?

Genesis 37:31-35 (KJV)
31 And they took Joseph's coat, and killed a kid of the goats, and dipped the coat in the blood;
32 And they sent the coat of many colours, and they brought it to their father; and said, This have we found: know now whether it be thy son's coat or no.
33 And he knew it, and said, It is my son's coat; an evil beast hath devoured him; Joseph is without doubt rent in pieces.

34 And Jacob rent his clothes, and put sackcloth upon his loins, and mourned for his son many days.

35 And all his sons and all his daughters rose up to comfort him; but he refused to be comforted; and he said, For I will go down into the grave unto my son mourning. Thus his father wept for him.

Genesis 41:41-43 (KJV)

41 And Pharaoh said unto Joseph, See, I have set thee over all the land of Egypt.

42 And Pharaoh took off his ring from his hand, and put it upon Joseph's hand, and arrayed him in vestures of fine linen, and put a gold chain about his neck;

43 And he made him to ride in the second chariot which he had; and they cried before him, Bow the knee: and he made him ruler over all the land of Egypt.

Genesis 45:1-5 (KJV)

1Then Joseph could not refrain himself before all them that stood by him; and he cried, Cause every man to go out from me. And there stood no man with him, while Joseph made himself known unto his brethren.

2 And he wept aloud: and the Egyptians and the house of Pharaoh heard.

3 And Joseph said unto his brethren, I am Joseph; doth my father yet live? And his brethren could not answer him; for they were troubled at his presence.

4 And Joseph said unto his brethren, Come near to me, I pray you. And they came near. And he said, I am Joseph your brother, whom ye sold into Egypt.

5 Now therefore be not grieved, nor angry with yourselves, that ye sold me hither: for God did send me before you to preserve life.

Dr. Lydia A. Woods

Just Do It!

Mark 16:15-20 (KJV)

Mark 16:15-20 (KJV)

15 And he said unto them, Go ye into all the world, and preach the gospel to every creature.

16 He that believeth and is baptized shall be saved; but he that believeth not shall be damned.

17 And these signs shall follow them that believe; In my name shall they cast out devils; they shall speak with new tongues;

18 They shall take up serpents; and if they drink any deadly thing, it shall not hurt them; they shall lay hands on the sick, and they shall recover.

19 So then after the Lord had spoken unto them, he was received up into heaven, and sat on the right hand of God.

20 And they went forth, and preached every where, the Lord working with them, and confirming the word with signs following. Amen.

Just Give It!

Acts 20:35; Luke 6:34-38 (KJV)

Acts 20:35 (KJV)

[35] I have shewed you all things, how that so labouring ye ought to support the weak, and to remember the words of the Lord Jesus, how he said, It is more blessed to give than to receive.

Luke 6:34-38 (KJV)

[34] And if ye lend to them of whom ye hope to receive, what thank have ye? for sinners also lend to sinners, to receive as much again.

[35] But love ye your enemies, and do good, and lend, hoping for nothing again; and your reward shall be great, and ye shall be the children of the Highest: for he is kind unto the unthankful and to the evil.

[36] Be ye therefore merciful, as your Father also is merciful.

[37] Judge not, and ye shall not be judged: condemn not, and ye shall not be condemned: forgive, and ye shall be forgiven:

[38] Give, and it shall be given unto you; good measure, pressed down, and shaken together, and running over, shall men give into your bosom. For with the same measure that ye mete withal it shall be measured to you again.

Dr. Lydia A. Woods

Just Wait!

Psalms 25:3; 27:14; 37:18; Isaiah 40:31 (KJV)

Psalms 25:3 (KJV)
3 Yea, let none that wait on thee be ashamed: let them be ashamed which transgress without cause.

Psalms 27:14 (KJV)
14 Wait on the Lord be of good courage, and he shall strengthen thine heart: wait, I say, on the Lord.

Psalms 37:18 (KJV)
18 The Lord knoweth the days of the upright: and their inheritance shall be for ever.

Isaiah 40:31 (KJV)
31 But they that wait upon the Lord shall renew their strength; they shall mount up with wings as eagles; they shall run, and not be weary; and they shall walk, and not faint.

Lean Not

Proverbs 3:5-6; James 1:5 (KJV)

Proverbs 3:5-6 (KJV)
5 Trust in the Lord with all thine heart; and lean not unto thine own understanding.
6 In all thy ways acknowledge him, and he shall direct thy paths.

James 1:5 (KJV)
5 If any of you lack wisdom, let him ask of God, that giveth to all men liberally, and upbraideth not; and it shall be given him.

Dr. Lydia A. Woods

Master of Masters

Matthew 4:1, 4:19, 5:1, 7:29, 8:26, 11:5; Luke 8:43-48; John 2:1-11, 11:43-44 (KJV)

Matthew 4:1 (KJV)
1 Then was Jesus led up of the Spirit into the wilderness to be tempted of the devil.

Matthew 4:19 (KJV)
19 And he saith unto them, Follow me, and I will make you fishers of men.

Matthew 5:1 (KJV)
1 And seeing the multitudes, he went up into a mountain: and when he was set, his disciples came unto him:

Matthew 7:29 (KJV)
29 For he taught them as one having authority, and not as the scribes.

Matthew 8:26 (KJV)
26 And he saith unto them, Why are ye fearful, O ye of little faith? Then he arose, and rebuked the winds and the sea; and there was a great calm.

Matthew 11:5 (KJV)
5 The blind receive their sight, and the lame walk, the lepers are cleansed, and the deaf hear, the dead are raised up, and the poor have the gospel preached to them.

Luke 8:43-48 (KJV)
43 And a woman having an issue of blood twelve years, which had spent all her living upon physicians, neither could be healed of any,
44 Came behind him, and touched the border of his garment: and immediately her issue of blood stanched.

45 And Jesus said, Who touched me? When all denied, Peter and they that were with him said, Master, the multitude throng thee and press thee, and sayest thou, Who touched me?

46 And Jesus said, Somebody hath touched me: for I perceive that virtue is gone out of me.

47 And when the woman saw that she was not hid, she came trembling, and falling down before him, she declared unto him before all the people for what cause she had touched him, and how she was healed immediately.

48 And he said unto her, Daughter, be of good comfort: thy faith hath made thee whole; go in peace.

John 2:1-11 (KJV)

1 And the third day there was a marriage in Cana of Galilee; and the mother of Jesus was there:

2 And both Jesus was called, and his disciples, to the marriage.

3 And when they wanted wine, the mother of Jesus saith unto him, They have no wine.

4 Jesus saith unto her, Woman, what have I to do with thee? mine hour is not yet come.

5 His mother saith unto the servants, Whatsoever he saith unto you, do it.

6 And there were set there six waterpots of stone, after the manner of the purifying of the Jews, containing two or three firkins apiece.

7 Jesus saith unto them, Fill the waterpots with water. And they filled them up to the brim.

8 And he saith unto them, Draw out now, and bear unto the governor of the feast. And they bare it.

Dr. Lydia A. Woods

9 When the ruler of the feast had tasted the water that was made wine, and knew not whence it was: (but the servants which drew the water knew;) the governor of the feast called the bridegroom,
10 And saith unto him, Every man at the beginning doth set forth good wine; and when men have well drunk, then that which is worse: but thou hast kept the good wine until now.
11 This beginning of miracles did Jesus in Cana of Galilee, and manifested forth his glory; and his disciples believed on him.

John 11:43-44 (KJV)
43 And when he thus had spoken, he cried with a loud voice, Lazarus, come forth.
44 And he that was dead came forth, bound hand and foot with graveclothes: and his face was bound about with a napkin. Jesus saith unto them, Loose him, and let him go.

Master of Masters

The Perfect Murder

Romans 7:14-21 (KJV)

Romans 7:14-21 (KJV)

14 For we know that the law is spiritual: but I am carnal, sold under sin.

15 For that which I do I allow not: for what I would, that do I not; but what I hate, that do I.

16 If then I do that which I would not, I consent unto the law that it is good.

17 Now then it is no more I that do it, but sin that dwelleth in me.

18 For I know that in me (that is, in my flesh,) dwelleth no good thing: for to will is present with me; but how to perform that which is good I find not.

19 For the good that I would I do not: but the evil which I would not, that I do.

20 Now if I do that I would not, it is no more I that do it, but sin that dwelleth in me.

21 I find then a law, that, when I would do good, evil is present with me.

Resistance is Futile

1 Corinthians 6:17, 12:12-27 (KJV)

1 Corinthians 6:17 (KJV)
17 But he that is joined unto the Lord is one spirit.

1 Corinthians 12:12-27 (KJV)
12 For as the body is one, and hath many members, and all the members of that one body, being many, are one body: so also is Christ.

13 For by one Spirit are we all baptized into one body, whether we be Jews or Gentiles, whether we be bond or free; and have been all made to drink into one Spirit.

14 For the body is not one member, but many.

15 If the foot shall say, Because I am not the hand, I am not of the body; is it therefore not of the body?

16 And if the ear shall say, Because I am not the eye, I am not of the body; is it therefore not of the body?

17 If the whole body were an eye, where were the hearing? If the whole were hearing, where were the smelling?

18 But now hath God set the members every one of them in the body, as it hath pleased him.

19 And if they were all one member, where were the body?

20 But now are they many members, yet but one body.

21 And the eye cannot say unto the hand, I have no need of thee: nor again the head to the feet, I have no need of you.

22 Nay, much more those members of the body, which seem to be more feeble, are necessary:

23 And those members of the body, which we think to be less honourable, upon these we bestow more abundant honour; and our uncomely parts have more abundant comeliness.

24 For our comely parts have no need: but God hath tempered the body together, having given more abundant honour to that part which lacked.

25 That there should be no schism in the body; but that the members should have the same care one for another.

26 And whether one member suffer, all the members suffer with it; or one member be honoured, all the members rejoice with it.

27 Now ye are the body of Christ, and members in particular.

Resistance is Futile

Seeds of Self-Destruction

James 1:26, 3:5-10; Proverbs 18:21, 25:23 (KJV)

James 1:26 (KJV)

26 If any man among you seem to be religious, and bridleth not his tongue, but deceiveth his own heart, this man's religion is vain.

James 3:5-10 (KJV)

5 Even so the tongue is a little member, and boasteth great things. Behold, how great a matter a little fire kindleth!

6 And the tongue is a fire, a world of iniquity: so is the tongue among our members, that it defileth the whole body, and setteth on fire the course of nature; and it is set on fire of hell.

7 For every kind of beasts, and of birds, and of serpents, and of things in the sea, is tamed, and hath been tamed of mankind:

8 But the tongue can no man tame; it is an unruly evil, full of deadly poison.

9 Therewith bless we God, even the Father; and therewith curse we men, which are made after the similitude of God.

10 Out of the same mouth proceedeth blessing and cursing. My brethren, these things ought not so to be.

Proverbs 18:21 (KJV)

21 Death and life are in the power of the tongue: and they that love it shall eat the fruit thereof.

Proverbs 25:23 (KJV)

23 The north wind driveth away rain: so doth an angry countenance a backbiting tongue.

Simply Because You Are Mine

Matthew 7:11; 1 Corinthians 2:9-11; Isaiah 64:4;
Psalms 31:19 (KJV)

Matthew 7:11 (KJV)
[11] If ye then, being evil, know how to give good gifts unto your children, how much more shall your Father which is in heaven give good things to them that ask him?

1 Corinthians 2:9-11 (KJV)
[9] But as it is written, Eye hath not seen, nor ear heard, neither have entered into the heart of man, the things which God hath prepared for them that love him.
[10] But God hath revealed them unto us by his Spirit: for the Spirit searcheth all things, yea, the deep things of God.
[11] For what man knoweth the things of a man, save the spirit of man which is in him? even so the things of God knoweth no man, but the Spirit of God.

Isaiah 64:4 (KJV)
[4] For since the beginning of the world men have not heard, nor perceived by the ear, neither hath the eye seen, O God, beside thee, what he hath prepared for him that waiteth for him.

Psalms 31:19 (KJV)
[19] Oh how great is thy goodness, which thou hast laid up for them that fear thee; which thou hast wrought for them that trust in thee before the sons of men!

So Be Like Job

Job 1:1, 8-12; 2:1-6; 42:12-13 (KJV)

Job 1:1 (KJV)

[1] There was a man in the land of Uz, whose name was Job; and that man was perfect and upright, and one that feared God, and eschewed evil.

Job 1:8-12 (KJV)

[8] And the Lord said unto Satan, Hast thou considered my servant Job, that there is none like him in the earth, a perfect and an upright man, one that feareth God, and escheweth evil?

[9] Then Satan answered the Lord, and said, Doth Job fear God for nought?

[10] Hast not thou made an hedge about him, and about his house, and about all that he hath on every side? thou hast blessed the work of his hands, and his substance is increased in the land.

[11] But put forth thine hand now, and touch all that he hath, and he will curse thee to thy face.

[12] And the Lord said unto Satan, Behold, all that he hath is in thy power; only upon himself put not forth thine hand. So Satan went forth from the presence of the Lord.

Job 2:1-6 (KJV)

[1] Again there was a day when the sons of God came to present themselves before the Lord, and Satan came also among them to present himself before the Lord.

[2] And the Lord said unto Satan, From whence comest thou? And Satan answered the Lord, and said, From going to and fro in the earth, and from walking up and down in it.

³ And the Lord said unto Satan, Hast thou considered my servant Job, that there is none like him in the earth, a perfect and an upright man, one that feareth God, and escheweth evil? and still he holdeth fast his integrity, although thou movedst me against him, to destroy him without cause.
⁴ And Satan answered the Lord, and said, Skin for skin, yea, all that a man hath will he give for his life.
⁵ But put forth thine hand now, and touch his bone and his flesh, and he will curse thee to thy face.
⁶ And the Lord said unto Satan, Behold, he is in thine hand; but save his life.

Job 42:12-13 (KJV)
¹² So the Lord blessed the latter end of Job more than his beginning: for he had fourteen thousand sheep, and six thousand camels, and a thousand yoke of oxen, and a thousand she asses.
¹³ He had also seven sons and three daughters.

Dr. Lydia A. Woods

So Great a Cloud of Witnesses

Hebrews 12:1 (KJV)

Hebrews 12:1 (KJV)
[1] Wherefore seeing we also are compassed about with so great a cloud of witnesses, let us lay aside every weight, and the sin which doth so easily beset us, and let us run with patience the race that is set before us,

Somethin' Told Me

John 12:26; Ephesians 4:30; Luke 2:26 (KJV)

John 12:26 (KJV)
26 If any man serve me, let him follow me; and where I am, there shall also my servant be: if any man serve me, him will my Father honour.

Ephesians 4:30 (KJV)
30 And grieve not the holy Spirit of God, whereby ye are sealed unto the day of redemption.

Luke 2:26 (KJV)
26 And it was revealed unto him by the Holy Ghost, that he should not see death, before he had seen the Lord's Christ.

Dr. Lydia A. Woods

Take No Thought

Luke 12:22-30 (KJV)

Luke 12:22-30 (KJV)

22 And he said unto his disciples, Therefore I say unto you, Take no thought for your life, what ye shall eat; neither for the body, what ye shall put on.

23 The life is more than meat, and the body is more than raiment.

24 Consider the ravens: for they neither sow nor reap; which neither have storehouse nor barn; and God feedeth them: how much more are ye better than the fowls?

25 And which of you with taking thought can add to his stature one cubit?

26 If ye then be not able to do that thing which is least, why take ye thought for the rest?

27 Consider the lilies how they grow: they toil not, they spin not; and yet I say unto you, that Solomon in all his glory was not arrayed like one of these.

28 If then God so clothe the grass, which is to day in the field, and to morrow is cast into the oven; how much more will he clothe you, O ye of little faith?

29 And seek not ye what ye shall eat, or what ye shall drink, neither be ye of doubtful mind.

30 For all these things do the nations of the world seek after: and your Father knoweth that ye have need of these things.

There But For the Grace...

Luke 10:27-37; Matthew 22:39 (KJV)

Luke 10:27-37 (KJV)

27 And he answering said, Thou shalt love the Lord thy God with all thy heart, and with all thy soul, and with all thy strength, and with all thy mind; and thy neighbour as thyself.

28 And he said unto him, Thou hast answered right: this do, and thou shalt live.

29 But he, willing to justify himself, said unto Jesus, And who is my neighbour?

30 And Jesus answering said, A certain man went down from Jerusalem to Jericho, and fell among thieves, which stripped him of his raiment, and wounded him, and departed, leaving him half dead.

31 And by chance there came down a certain priest that way: and when he saw him, he passed by on the other side.

32 And likewise a Levite, when he was at the place, came and looked on him, and passed by on the other side.

33 But a certain Samaritan, as he journeyed, came where he was: and when he saw him, he had compassion on him,

34 And went to him, and bound up his wounds, pouring in oil and wine, and set him on his own beast, and brought him to an inn, and took care of him.

35 And on the morrow when he departed, he took out two pence, and gave them to the host, and said unto him, Take care of him; and whatsoever thou spendest more, when I come again, I will repay thee.

36 Which now of these three, thinkest thou, was neighbour unto him that fell among the thieves?

37 And he said, He that shewed mercy on him. Then said Jesus unto him, Go, and do thou likewise.

Matthew 22:39 (KJV)
39 And the second is like unto it, Thou shalt love thy neighbour as thyself.

True Way of Life
John 13:34-35, 14:6 (KJV)

John 13:34-35 (KJV)
34 A new commandment I give unto you, That ye love one another; as I have loved you, that ye also love one another.
35 By this shall all men know that ye are my disciples, if ye have love one to another.

John 14:6 (KJV)
6 Jesus saith unto him, I am the way, the truth, and the life: no man cometh unto the Father, but by me.

What's His Face?

Genesis 3:15; John 19:11 (KJV)

Genesis 3:15 (KJV)

15 And I will put enmity between thee and the woman, and between thy seed and her seed; it shall bruise thy head, and thou shalt bruise his heel.

John 19:11 (KJV)

11 Jesus answered, Thou couldest have no power at all against me, except it were given thee from above: therefore he that delivered me unto thee hath the greater sin.

With His Own Blood

Acts 20:28; Hosea 2:19; Revelation 19:7-9; 21:9 (KJV)

Acts 20:28 (KJV)

28 Take heed therefore unto yourselves, and to all the flock, over the which the Holy Ghost hath made you overseers, to feed the church of God, which he hath purchased with his own blood.

Hosea 2:19 (KJV)

19 And I will betroth thee unto me for ever; yea, I will betroth thee unto me in righteousness, and in judgment, and in lovingkindness, and in mercies.

Revelation 19:7-9 (KJV)

7 Let us be glad and rejoice, and give honour to him: for the marriage of the Lamb is come, and his wife hath made herself ready.
8 And to her was granted that she should be arrayed in fine linen, clean and white: for the fine linen is the righteousness of saints.
9 And he saith unto me, Write, Blessed are they which are called unto the marriage supper of the Lamb. And he saith unto me, These are the true sayings of God.

Revelation 21:9 (KJV)

9 And there came unto me one of the seven angels which had the seven vials full of the seven last plagues, and talked with me, saying, Come hither, I will shew thee the bride, the Lamb's wife.

Scriptural
Index

128:3
Generations in You, 100
Proverbs
3:5-6
Lean Not, 129
16:16-25
The Gift, 101
18:21
Seeds of Self-Destruction, 136
19:21
If You Want to Make God
Laugh!, 115
25:23
Seeds of Self-Destruction, 136
Isaiah
40:31
Just Wait!, 128
46:9-11
If You Want to Make God
Laugh!, 115
64:4
Simply Because You Are Mine,
137
Hosea
2:19
With His Own Blood, 147
Matthew
4:1
Master of Masters, 130
4:19
Master of Masters, 130
5:1
Master of Masters, 130
5:36
If You Want to Make God
Laugh!, 115

7:11
Simply Because You Are Mine,
137
7:29
Master of Masters, 130
8:26
Master of Masters, 130
11:5
Master of Masters, 130
21:24
A Bible Character, 92
22:39
There But For the Grace..., 143
Mark
11:25-26
Forgive or Forgive Not, 99
15:1
A Bible Character, 92
13:24-27
Good News, 108
15:10-11
A Bible Character, 92
16:1
A Bible Character, 92
16:15-20
Just Do It!, 126
Luke
2:7
God's M.O., 107
2:26
Somethin' Told Me, 141
4:1-13
If Thou Be..., 114
6:34-38
Just Give it!, 127
6:37
Forgive or Forgive Not, 99

Dr. Lydia A. Woods